The Poetic Art of
Nissim Ezekiel

The Poetic Art of
Nissim Ezekiel

Sanjit Mishra

ATLANTIC
PUBLISHERS & DISTRIBUTORS (P) LTD

Published by

ATLANTIC

PUBLISHERS & DISTRIBUTORS (P) LTD

7/22, Ansari Road, Darya Ganj,
New Delhi-110002
Phones : +91-11-40775252, 23273880, 23275880, 23280451
Fax : +91-11-23285873
Web : www.atlanticbooks.com
E-mail : orders@atlanticbooks.com

Branch Office
5, Nallathambi Street, Wallajah Road,
Chennai-600002
Phones : +91-44-64611085, 32413319
E-mail : chennai@atlanticbooks.com

Printed in India at Nice Printing Press, A-33/3A, Site-IV, Industrial Area, Sahibabad, Ghaziabad, U.P.

IN MEMORIAM

SHRI AKHILANAND MISHRA

My Maternal Grandfather

Who

Initiated Me into the World of Letters

PREFACE

Nissim Ezekiel is one of those few men of letters who become legends in their life-time by virtue of their creative and critical potentialities as manifested in their writings. A dramatist of known credentials, a literary critic of encyclopaedic range and an acknowledged academician in his own rights, Ezekiel will, however, be remembered primarily as a poet. His poetic career spans a period of over half-a-century which saw the publication of about three hundred poems comprising eight volumes including the epoch making book, *A Time to Change* which introduced, in a way, the Modernist element in Indian poetry in English. With the publication of the *Collected Poems* (1989), the poet in him seems to have reaped a rich harvest, and it is appropriate that his expanding poetic sensibility should now be evaluated in its totality to place him in the galaxy of modern poets.

A review of critical literature on him demonstrates that the three book-length studies that have appeared so far have not taken into account the whole gamut of his poetic personality in all its complexity. Chetan Karnani's *Nissim Ezekiel* (1974), obviously ignores the poet's two major volumes, *Hymns in Darkness* and the Akademi award winning title *Latter-Day Psalms* which were published much later. Anisur Rahman's *Form and Value in the Poetry of Nissim Ezekiel* (1981) also suffers from a similar handicap in that it excludes Ezekiel's latest poems. The third and last addition is Harish Raizada's *Nissim Ezekiel : A Poet of Human Balance* (1992) which concentrates simply on the humanistic preoccupations which form just a fraction of Ezekiel's poetic virtuosity. Among critical anthologies, Prof. Surya Nath Pandey's recently published *Nissim Ezekiel : Dimensions of a Poetic Genius* (1999) is a salutary collection of perceptive essay, though it does not provide a systematic graph of Ezekiel's poetic development for obvious reasons. The present volume seeks to fill in a serious gap in Ezekiel scholarship.

Executed in six chapters, the work opens with "Introduction," which has three sections dealing with a brief survey of Indian poetry in English, Ezekiel's biographical sketch, and the formative influences on him respectively. Ezekiel's poetic creed has been dealt with in the second chapter which exhaustively analyses his views on poetry and the poetic process. Ezekiel's poetry has been examined in three well-marked phases — the Romantic, the Realist and the Humanist in three separate chapters. Chapter III is devoted to the analysis of his Romantic Phase beginning with the composition of his "Early Poems" in 1945 and ends in 1958. It includes the poems published in *A Time to Change, Sixty Poems* and *The Third*. The theme of love, the problem of identity and self questioning are the recurring concerns of this phase.

The middle phase of Ezekiel's career forms the content of the fourth chapter titled "The Realist Phase" and covers the years between 1959-1976. This is the poet's richest phase in terms of creative output as it saw the publication of *The Unfinished Man, The Exact Name* and *Hymns in Darkness*. Ezekiel's famous anthology-pieces like "Night of Scorpion," "Background, Casually," "Island" and "Goodbye Party for Miss Pushpa, T.S." belong to this phase. The sense of belonging to his roots, a commitment to the native situation, and a realistic portrayal are the hallmarks of this period. The fifth chapter is devoted to an analysis of Ezekiel's recent phase commencing since 1977 till date and is christened as the Humanist phase. The poems discussed include those in *Latter-day Psalms* and the "Latest Poems" in *Collected Poems* (1989). This phase demonstrates a different perspective in that the poet looks at the macrocosm with an unusual joy and celebrates life despite transitoriness and fallibility. To a perceptive reader, his attitude betrays the typical Indian trait of *Vasudhaika Kutumbakam* (the whole world as family). The earlier ironic bite and satirical exposure acquire a milder tone and sympathetic colour in this phase.

The final achievement of the poet has been estimated in the concluding chapter. Ezekiel's poetic graph evidences a poetic talent relentlessly endeavouring to define self in terms of surrounding realities. The instinctive awareness of marginality equipped him to dilate on the native situation dispassionately and uninhibitedly.

Cultural anguish and anxiety which pervade his early poetry finally yield to an unusual sense of acceptance and affirmation. By coming to terms with his surroundings the angry individualist in Ezekiel acquires a serenity and calmness that endows him with an enlarged imaginative sympathy. The post-colonial Indian poetry in English owes much to Ezekiel for creative versatility, critical insight and poetic craftsmanship.

SANJIT MISHRA

ACKNOWLEDGMENTS

It is my privilege to acknowledge the blessings of my teacher Dr. Surya Nath Pandey, Professor of English, Banaras Hindu University, whose guidance has ever been my great strength in the trying moments of life. Words are simply inadequate to express my gratitude to him. I recall with reverence the good wishes of my dear parents for my academic pursuits. My younger brothers Ajit and Ritesh deserve my love for their affectionate encouragements.

SANJIT MISHRA

CONTENTS

1
Introduction

I

Given its unique capacity to assimilate divergent mores India has adopted various languages with perfect ease and equanimity over the centuries. The important acquisition among them is English, the language of our British colonisers. It has almost been naturalised as a popular medium of expression by a number of Indian poets, novelists, dramatists and essayists who claim parity with their counterparts in the English speaking countries of the world. Despite the raised eye-brows and frowning faces of the votaries of *Swadeshi* questioning the efficiency of English as a suitable medium to depict the Indian situation, we have a galaxy of litterateurs like Mulk Raj Anand, R.K. Narayan, Raja Rao, Nirad C. Chaudhury, Nissim Ezekiel, A.K. Ramanujan, Dom Moraes, Vikram Seth, the Booker-awardee Arundhati Roy and the Pulitzer Prize-winner Jhumpa Lahiri who have canonised Indian Writing in English as a vital component of Commonwealth literature.

This spectacular emergence of Indian writing in English has a long history which dates back to the colonial times when English used to be the language of British rulers and a few aristocratic Indians who were deeply (and flatteringly also) enthralled by this language of their subjugators. Apart from the English writings which appeared in prose, the earliest attempt in the field of poetry was made in 1825 by Cavelly Venkata Ramaswami who translated into English Arasanipala Venkatadhvarin's *Viswagunadarsana*. Henry Louis Vivian Derozio (1809-31) is credited as the first Indian poet in English who brought out two volumes in verse-

Poems (1827) and *The Fakeer of Jungheera : A Memorial Tale and Other Poems* (1828), which demonstrates his strong affinity with Byron. His shorter pieces like "To India — My Native Land," "The Harp of India" and "To the Pupils of Hindu College" have "an unmistakable authenticity of patriotic utterance which stamps Derozio as an Indian English poet who is truly a son of the soil."[1] He initiated a tradition of writing poetry in English which can be easily divided in two phases — the pre-Independence and the post-Independence. Derozio, Kashiprasad Ghose, Rajnarain Dutt and Michael Madhusudan Dutt are among the significant poets of the earlier part of the pre-Independence phase.

After the great mutiny of 1857 rightly regarded by many as the first war of Independence, and the atrocities heaped upon the revolutionaries, there was an upsurge of nationalistic fervour among Indians. Fired with a patriotic zeal some Indians like Swami Dayanand Saraswati and Vivekanand took to reawakening the nationalistic spirit among countrymen to repudiate the false notion of British superiority and to assert the glorious past of India. While on the other hand, there were others who were swayed by the British pelf and power and pledged themselves to the English. Not only were they attracted to their political or social positions, but most of them proselytized themselves to Christianity also. To this period and group belong the Dutts — Govind Chander, Hur Chander, Girish Chander, Umesh Chander, Toru and Aru — and Man Mohan Ghose who was the elder brother of Sri Aurobindo. *The Dutt Family Album* (1870) comprising poems by the members of the Dutt family recently converted to Christianity betray their slavish attitude to everything that was British. Another poet Nobo Kissen Ghose known as Ram Sharma (1837-1918), on the other hand, wrote with some genuineness and authenticity and can be considered as the first mystic poet of Indian English poetry. His volumes include *Willow Drops, The Last Day : A Poem* and *Miscellaneous Poems*. His poetry, however, hangs between two extremes — at the one end he shows admiration for the British rulers while on the other he praises nationalists like Swami Vivekanand. Ram Sharma was extremely overpowered by the love for the West to the extent of expressing his responses to the Indian experiences through the myths of the West.

Besides a few other poets of lesser repute, the achievements of Romesh Chander Dutt (1848-1909), a nephew of Govind Chander Dutt, and Man Mohan Ghose (1869-1924) are also quite significant. Romesh Chander's output lies mainly in his translation of the *Ramayana* and the *Mahabharata* in English. Man Mohan Ghose is considered to be the most talented of these poets. His poetry is a product of his cultural alienation which stifled his interest in India owing to his education in England. His works include *Primavera* (which was published in collaboration with Stephen Phillips, Lawrence Binyon, and Arthur Cripps), *Love Songs and Elegies*, *Songs of Love and Death* and *Orphic Mysteries and Immortal Eve.*

Toru Dutt (1856-77), the younger cousin of Romesh Chander and the youngest daughter of Govind Chander Dutt was the most gifted poet of this phase. A tender hearted girl that she was, her poetic output would have been rare had she only been allotted a little longer span of life. Like Ram Sharma's, hers also was a similar attitude of ambivalence towards Britain and loved the British ways yet she had a penchant for the Indian mythology. It is a very curious fact that though she was a Christian convert, she had deep love for Indian legends and classics. She has extensively exploited some of the native myths and legends in her *Ancient Ballads and Legends of Hindustan*, which was posthumously published in 1882. M.K. Naik's evaluation of her achievement is too pertinent to be overlooked :

> What is most impressive about Toru Dutt's poetry is its virtually total freedom from imitation (in contrast with Kashiprasad Ghose and M.M. Dutt) at an age when most writers are in their artistic swaddling clothes.... Her best work has the qualities of a quiet strength, of deep emotion held under artistic restraint and an acute awareness of the abiding values of Indian life (*A History of Indian English Literature*, pp. 40-41).

The later phase of pre-Independence poetry includes the grand names like Rabindranath Tagore, Sri Aurobindo and Sarojini Naidu who were entirely different from their predecessors in that theirs is a maturer poetry both thematically and stylistically. Tinged with nationalistic sentiments, they show some involvement in the contemporary political scene which was steeped in freedom movement. Rabindranath Tagore (1861-1941) was basically a Bangla poet but his own translation of *Gitanjali* won him the coveted Nobel Prize in 1913. It was followed by *The Gardener*, *The Crescent Moon*, *Stray Birds* and *The Fugitive*. *Gitanjali's* motto "I am here to sing thee songs" sums up the basic spiritual content of Tagore's poetry. He sees God as "unbroken perfection" and has endeavoured to express His glory in mystical terms. Unlike his elder brother Man Mohan Ghose, Sri Aurobindo (1872-1950) was a hardcore nationalist who had deep love for India and aspired to its freedom. His intellectual development has four milestones-patriot, poet, yogi, seer — which form at once his strength and weakness. Comprising twelve books, his *magnum opus*, *Savitri* is a poem of staggering dimensions. This deeply philosophical Hindu epic has 'metred the rhythm-beats of eternity' and Prof. Iyengar compares it with Dante's well-known masterpiece :

> In a sense, *Savitri* is *The Life Divine* turned into poetry even as the *Divine Comedy* is Catholic theology and the philosophy of St. Thomas Aquinas given a poetic body. Nevertheless, it needs to be reiterated that *Savitri* and the Divine Comedy are significant poetry, not mere philosophy or theology dressed up in poetical fripperies.[2]

Sarojini Naidu (1879-1949) was an equally talented poet whose artistic gifts clashed with her political involvement. Before participating in social activities, she had brought out her first volume *The Golden Threshold* which was followed by *The Birth of Time*, *The Broken Wing*, and the collected poems, *The Sceptered Flute*. Her finest lyrics have a perfect structure and a rare craftsmanship. However, since her diction and imagery are derived from conventional romantic sources, her work appears to be irretrievably outdated by the parametres of modern poetics. Her contribution lies in giving an authentic Indian English utterance marvellously tuned to the composite Indian ethos marked by the splendours of native scenario. Her younger brother Harindra Nath Chattopadhyaya wrote more prolifically as his poetic span expands for seven decades. His collections include *The Feast of Youth*, *The Magic Tree*, *Spring in Winter* and *Virgins and Vineyards*.

The pre-Independence poets, thus, have dealt with a variety of themes and styles. While Derozio used a derivative and romantic style, Romesh Chander Dutt had a narrative style, Michael Madhusudan Dutt's was an epical one, Toru Dutt's simple and transparent while Tagore used prose-poem style, Man Mohan Ghose imitated the style of the decadents of the naughty Nineties, Sri Aurobindo dealt with a somewhat obscure and *Mantrik* style, Naidu's technique is sophisticated and figurative. The poetry of pre-Independence era basically has a social and political orientation. It is also to be noted that in the initial stage, the Indian poets in English were imitators of the British Romantics in their style but since 1857, nationalistic sentiments become part of their poetic design. The attainment of Independence in 1947 proved a turning point in the growth of Indian poetry in English. Bruce King has perceptively noted this phenomenon :

> Unlike the creative writing of Africa and the Caribbean, modern Indian poetry in English has been neglected by most critics, foreign readers and intellectuals for it has no obvious direct relationship to the cultural movements which led to national independence; by 1947 the situation had changed and with it the concern of the new poets became their relationship to and alienation from the realities of their society.[3]

The Indians writing poetry in English accepted the challenge thrown up by some critics that English was simply inadequate to express the Indian situation in all its multiplicity. This modern poetry in English grew some more teeth and got poised to meet such demands with practitioners like Kamala Das who asserted her freedom to choose a language for creative expression :

> The language I speak
> Becomes mine, its distortions, its queernesses
> All mine, mine alone. It is half English, half
> Indian, funny perhaps, but it is honest
> It is as human as I am human,...[4]

The poets of this phase — Nissim Ezekiel, Jayant Mahapatra, A.K. Ramanujan *et al.* — appeared self-confident while accepting English as their medium of expression. They turned their backs on the existing Romantic tradition and wrote poetry suited to the general temper of the times. These poets also tried to naturalise the modernistic elements propounded by Pound, Yeats and Eliot.

In 1958, P. Lal and his associates founded the Writers Workshop in Calcutta to promote the poetic efforts of these poets. It soon proved to be an effective forum for modernist poetry through its *Miscellany*, devoted to encouraging new and unpublished writers. In its seminal volume, *Modern Indo-Anglian Poetry* (1958), the editors vehemently attacked the poetry of Sri Aurobindo and others :

> It has spoilt a good deal of the Indo-Anglian Past; it can without exaggeration spell ruin for the future.... We claim that the phase of Indo-Anglian Romanticism ended with Sarojini Naidu... We must more and more aim at realistic poetry, reflecting poetically and pleasingly the din and hubub, the confusion and indecision, flashes of beauty and goodness of our age.... We emphasise the need for the private voice especially because we live in an age that tends so easily to demonstrations of mass approval and suited for a capsule minded public....[5]

Thus the poets of fifties and sixties started a search for an altogether new poetic idiom. The wild abstractions were replaced by concrete although somewhat complex images. This phase is characterised by experimentation and innovation, new imagery, authentic creative urge and superb craftsmanship. Pritish Nandy's observation is very precise and specific :

> After years of hortation and fruitless dialogue with eternity, long loud wails at the human predicament and garrulous search for the spiritual dimension to man's fate, the Indian poet in English decided to look into himself and search for his answers there. Not in terms of prophetic generalisations about god and the devil and all but in terms of the voiceless vacant in the still centre of the heart.[6]

Ezekiel with a host of poets who worked under his guidance saw to it that Indian Poetry in English is canonized as a major component of Commonwealth Poetry.

II

Nissim Ezekiel, a prominent poet of the post-Independence phase was born on 16 December 1924 to Moses Ezekiel Talkar and Diana of a Bene-Israel Jewish family in a chawl off the Byculla bridge in Bombay. His father was a Lecturer in Biology at Wilson College and mother was a teacher in a school founded by herself. Second among five brothers and sisters, Ezekiel was admitted to the Convent of Jesus and Mary, a school run by Christian missionaries. Later he sought admission to the Antonio D'souza High school of 'Background, Causally'[7] fame in 1934 and remained there until 1941. His classmates at the school included the Hindi film 'showman' Raj Kapoor, possibly one of "the strong/But undernourished Hindu lads" the poet refers to in his celebrated piece. It was in the summer of 1939 while vacationing at his grandfather's house in Tal, in rural Maharashtra that he read *Bhagavad Gita* in English translation. It is also possible that the most anthologized poem 'Night of the Scorpion' is based on the actual experience Ezekiel had during one of such visits to his ancestral village. The poet's interest in the Hindu texts at such a tender age was created by the school Fathers who criticised Hinduism unreservedly. In his interview with Frank Birbal Singh he dwells on the insular environment of his school :

> ... I was after all, in a Roman Catholic school, and the Fathers used to say to the students that there was nothing in Hinduism. The Hindus, Parsis, Muslims, all said, What? There is nothing in Hinduism? So we started reading the *Gita and the Upanishads* at school which I may not have done in the next ten years had the Fathers not said there was nothing in it.[8]

He joined the four-year BA course at the Presbyterian Wilson College and graduated in English Literature with a first class in the year 1945. Ezekiel joined the University of Bombay for post-graduation in English. He topped the list of successful students at the M.A. examination in 1947 and won the prestigious R.K. Lagu prize. So dynamic was Ezekiel's personality that while at Wilson College itself, he had joined M.N. Roy's Radical Democratic Party fighting for the cause of trade unionism. This contact with M.N.

Roy had a formative influence on Ezekiel's literary career and sharpened the humanistic edge of his personality :

> I've attempted to put into poetry as much as has happened to me. But actually what has gone into it is fairly limited, considering the time and energy spent on politics. I became a Royist at the age of 18. It went with rationalism, atheism, anti-religious convictions, the whole international movement which was partly Marxist-influenced. Indian society was to be made democratic, secular and scientific. That phase in my life lasted from 1942 to 1947, though I stopped being Royist in '51.[9]

He had begun composing poems while studying at Wilson College and his first piece was published in *Social Welfare* (1942), later on reprinted in the College's *The Wilsonian*. He also edited *The Student World* subsequently. His earliest surviving poem is "Exhortation" dated 13 December 1943, excluded from his *Collected Poems* and available in *Nissim Ezekiel : The Authorized Biography*.[10] Ezekiel spent a brief stint as a teacher of English literature at Khalsa College, Bombay from June 1947 to June 1948. He spent the rest of 1948 writing poetry, freelancing for newspapers and magazines.

This involvement in the Indian scene, however, could not hold Ezekiel for long. A deeper urge to see beyond the Indian horizons possibly goaded by a typical colonial mentality tempted Ezekiel to visit England. Fortunately his elderly friend Ebrahim Alkazi, a famous theatre personality, came to his help and arranged a one-way steamer ticket. Ezekiel sailed off in *Jal Azad* and reached London in November 1948 after undertaking a twenty-six day voyage at sea. Initially he stayed with Alkazi and took up a clerical post in the Internal Affairs Department of the Indian High Commission at London to partially meet his expenses there. Incidentally, his assignments included editing a weekly newsletter for the commission, a responsibility he loved to carry out even later in life, though mostly gratis. He registered for a B.A. in Philosophy at Birbeck College, affiliated to the University of London and studied under the legendary philosopher C.E.M. Joad about Plato, Aristotle and the Existentialists. However, he could not complete the course for want of time. Later he took the drastic decision to resign the job at India House to take to full time writing, earning a pound here and there by sending poems and reviews to British journals like *Strand Magazine*. He moved from Alkazi's flat and found accommodation in the basement of the same building immortalized in 'Background, Casually' — "Philosophy, /Poverty and Poetry, three/companions shared my basement room" (*CP*, p. 179).

In England Ezekiel met Keshav Malik, the first literary editor of *Thought*, a political journal started in 1948 in New Delhi, who was there to attend the inaugural meeting of the Congress for Cultural Freedom. Since Malik was also a follower of M.N. Roy's democratic socialism, they developed deep affinities for each other. With the publication of Ezekiel's poems in British literary journals, C.R. Mandy, the editor of *The Illustrated Weekly of India*, requested him to send his poems for publication back home as well. His interest in poetry remained predominant in his London sojourn despite financial stringencies and blossomed as *A Time to Change* (1952), his first book of poems published by the Fortune Press, London. It appears however, that Ezekiel had not only a tough time there which forced him to accept a clerical job in Indian High Commission but a shattering experience about achievements in a foreign country also. He alludes to this sense of failure — "I knew that I had failed / In everything, a bitter thought." Obviously, he felt like returning to his 'backward place' and arranged his return passage by accepting a menial job on a Cargo-ship bound for Indo-China. He boarded the ship in March 1952 and reached his 'Island' in May 1952.

Soon after his return, Ezekiel joined *The Illustrated Weekly of India* as an assistant editor and served there for two years. He also got associated with the All India Radio for ten years (1952-62) as a broadcaster on art and literature. On 23 November 1952 Ezekiel was married to Daisy Jacob at the Magen David Synagogue and this event forms the content of the poem "Jewish Wedding in Bombay." His second book of verse *Sixty Poems* (1953) was brought out by the Strand Bookshop, Bombay. The next year, he took to advertising with Shilpi Advertising concern as a copywriter. In the meanwhile his literary credentials got him appointed in 1955 as the first editor of the *Quest*. In 1956 Ezekiel visited America and stayed there for six months as the manager of the Shilpi. While staying in the States, he visited several American universities on a Farfield Foundation grant. His volume *The Third* was also published by Strand Bookshop in 1958. Ezekiel left the Shilpis in 1959 and joined as General Manager for picture-frame manufacturing company, Chemould where all the poems of *The Unfinished Man* (Writers Workshop, 1960) were written in a single year. Immediately after leaving Chemould, Ezekiel joined *Design* magazine as manager but stayed with them hardly for three months. In 1961, he got associated with *Imprint* as an associate editor in charge of the reviews section for seven years. This boosted Ezekiel's status as a critic of repute with his perceptive and influential criticism on literature, and arts. In June the same year, Ezekiel shifted back to the academics by accepting lectureship as well as the Headship of English department in Mithibai College of Arts, Vile Parle, Bombay and remained there for eleven long years. His junior colleagues there among others included R. Parthasarathy, the well-known Indian poet in English and this association seems to have been of great advantage to the development of post-colonial poetry in India. His connection with the *Indian Pen* started around 1952 and after serving in various capacities he took over as the editor of the journal after Madame Sophiya Wadia's death in April 1986. Even while teaching, he worked as art critic of *The Times of India* (1964-66) and delivered lecturers on Indian Writing in English at the University of Leeds as a Visiting Professor (January-June, 1964) His fourth volume *The Exact Name* was published by the Writers Workshop in 1965. He also began the *Poetry India* in 1966 which in its six issues took an account of modern poetry in various Indian languages.

In March 1967, Ezekiel visited America for the second time and stayed with A.K. Ramanujan at the University of Chicago. He held his sessions of poetry and delivered lectures in various universities on Indian Writing in English. April 1967 marks a significant milestone in his life as he took LSD trips for the first time which had a far-reaching impact on his poetry "a starting point for a self-transforming process," as he put it. Between 1967 and 1972 he had several LSD trips through which he rediscovered the divine aspect of life. However, they were replaced later on by various kinds of meditation and yoga.

Ezekiel's friendship with Ebrahim Alkazi attracted him towards theatre and in an interview he refers to the literary advantages of this intimacy :

> I became interested in the theatre through my association with E. Alkazi and his work in Bombay's Theatre Group. Later, we formed the Theatre Unit. To write plays became at that time a dream for me and to some extent it is still a dream. More than 15 years passed after my first 5 plays were written, and I regret the lapse but expect to make up for it before the end of 80's.[11]

In 1969, the Writers Workshop brought out his collection *Three Plays* (*Nalini, Marriage Poem* and *The Sleepwalkers*) and the journal *Enact* published *Song of Deprivation* in its July issue. His play, *Who Needs No Introduction*, written subsequently, is still unpublished. He also worked as the poetry editor of *The Illustrated Weekly* from 1969 to 1971. He moved on to the University of Bombay as Reader in American Literature in 1972 and was subsequently elevated to Professorship in 1978, a position he held until his superannuation in 1985. He was a 'radio and T.V. columnist' between the years 1973 and 1978. In collaboration with Vrinda Nabar he translated into English the Marathi work, *Snake-Skin and Other Poems of Indra Sant* in 1974. The same year, he went to America on a Cultural Exchange Programme of the Government of the United States and gave readings from his works besides seminars at several universities. His sixth poetic volume *Hymns in Darkness* was published by Oxford University Press in 1976. By now Ezekiel had achieved an international fame as a contemporary poet and the American periodical, *Journal of South Asian Literature* (1976) brought out a special issue on him. In 1976 Ezekiel attended the International Colloquium on the Inter-Cultural Encounters in Literature at the East-West Centre, Hawaii as a delegate with a Professional Associate Award. On home ground, he was honoured with the Excellence Award for his contribution to poetry on 30 April 1976. With the imposition of the Emergency in the mid-seventies, the publication of his journal *Quest* was stopped and he started editing *Freedom First*, a fortnightly devoted to literary and intellectual pursuits in 1977. Ezekiel was invited at Rotterdam International Poetry Festival for doing a poetry reading from 11-17 June 1978, where the poem "Latter-Day Psalm" was written.

A film *Picture a Poet*, scripted and directed by Jane Swamy, was premiered at the Alliance Francaise in Bombay in 1981. It begins with a voice-over of 'Background, Casually', the voice being Ezekiel's itself and shows him against the backdrop of the places associated with him including his desk at the PEN. Ezekiel's seventh volume of poems, *Latter-Day Psalms* (1982) won for him the Sahitya Akademi Award in 1983. (This volume has also been translated into Assamese.) He visited the Edinburgh Arts Festival in 1983 and read his poems at poetry reading sessions there. His *Edinburgh Interlude — Lightly*, that appeared in xeroxed form the same year, records his creative response to that event. In 1985, he went to Salzburg and a year later he attended the Frankfurt Book Fair in Germany besides visiting several other German cities doing readings and participating in the discussions that followed. He also chaired the international panel of judges for Commonwealth International Poetry Award in 1986. *Journal of Indian Writing in English* brought out its special Nissim Ezekiel issue the same year. In 1987, he visited Canada to attend the Conference 'India Forty Years after Independence' and also went to Hong Kong the same year. He was honoured with the coveted Padma Shri award by the Govt. of India for his 'Contribution to Literature in English' in 1988. He visited the New Zealand International Festival of Arts in 1988 and lectured at the Adelaid Book Fair, Australia and Wellington the same year. From December 1988 to March 1989, Ezekiel was invited to be poet-in-residence at the National University of Singapore. His unpublished poems in 'Singapore Sequence' are the product of this South-Asian experience. His *Collected Poems* (1952-1988) was brought out by Oxford University Press in 1989.

Ezekiel's prose writings appeared as *Selected Prose* in 1992. In February 1993, Ezekiel took a sixteen-day tour of England as a guest of the Arts Council of Great Britain. In December the same year, he spent two weeks in States for an American Jewish Joint Distribution Committee event. In between he was operated for hernia at a Bombay hospital. However, his literary activities continued unabated. Ezekiel visited the Banaras Hindu University to deliver the Professor Vikramaditya Rai Memorial Lecture on 'The Infinite Aspects of Critical Writing' on 6-7 September 1994. During his sojourn at Banaras, the present author had the privilege of accompanying this celebrity to the Buddhist pilgrim-centre at Sarnath as a post-graduate student. His last published creative work, the play *Don't Call It Suicide* appeared in 1994. One of his last articles 'Poetry in the Time of Tempests' was published in *Sunday Times* on 29 June 1997.

The symptoms of slow decline of Ezekiel's mental powers had appeared on many an occasion in the past, to the great worry of his friends, admirers, students and the family members. He unfortunately collapsed at an American Jewish Joint Distribution Committee meeting in Bombay in August 1998 and had to be hospitalized at the Shushruta Nursing Home at Dadar. He was diagnosed as suffering from Alzheimer's disease. In October the same year, he was shifted to the A.J. Dias Nursing Home at Turner Road, Bandra (Bombay) where he has been struggling for life till date (*i.e.,* February 2001 when this manuscript is being prepared). Ironically enough in one of his sixties poems 'A Small Summit,' Ezekiel plans to go his way :

> ... be my own guest in my own
> one-man lunatic asylum,
> questioning the Furies, my patron saints
> about their old and new obscurities.
>
> (*CP*, p. 153)

In view of the fact that Dias Nursing Home Houses mentally-deranged persons and destitutes, Ezekiel's metaphor of alienation has taken on a literal denotation.

III

Every writer is a typical product of his age and the literary movements prevailing at the time substantially affect his works. Nissim Ezekiel has palpably been influenced by the contemporary poets like T.S. Eliot, W.B. Yeats, Ezra Pound and Philip Larkin. These influences shaped his creative odyssey that stretches well over five decades. In fact, the huge bulk of his writings, creative as well as critical, evidences a receptive personality prone to assimilate various impacts. To Suresh Kohli's query as to who were his early influences, Ezekiel replied :

> Some of my early poetry was influenced by Rilke. I did not succeed in assimilating this and eventually discarded it. I have imitated Eliot, Pound, Yeats and others, but never very well. My own voice has often been muffled or confused by random and temporary influences. That is the main weakness of my verse.... A clear influence is no proof of a poem's merit. Quite the contrary I was not influenced by Yeats after *The Unfinished Man*, nor by Eliot and Pound after *Sixty Poems*. I don't feel I make the grade to talk of influences at all. All this talk of influences may be of some value only when I write good poetry during the next ten years or so, which I certainly hope to do.[12]

Ezekiel's first two volumes *A Time to Change* and *Sixty Poems* bear a strong imprint of Rilke's mind. His poems like "Speech and Silence" and "Prayer I" appear to be written under Rilke's influence. The following lines bear testimony to this view :

> If I could pray, the gist of my
> Demanding would be simply this :
> Quietitude. The ordered mind.
> Erasure of the inner lie.
> And only love in every kiss.

("Prayer I", *CP*, p. 54)

Chetan Karnani has aptly noted this fact, "His early prayer was for quietitude. He wanted to seek the life of solitude and meditation. This ideal of Rilke is strongly expressed in these poems."[13] Ezekiel, however, denies having imbibed anything from Rilke straightway. He never intended to be a mere imitator :

> If someone were to say, "Ah, but in these poems in an early book there are echoes of Rilke and Eliot," I would agree. This does not mean that I produced a whole poem which is nothing but Rilke. If there were some poems like that, I don't think, I published them (*Selected Poems*, p. 171).

W.B. Yeats's is the most pronounced influence on Ezekiel's

early poetry which has derived immensely from the Irish poet's imagery and symbols. It was under Yeats's influence that Ezekiel identified parametres to discover his self at various stages of its development. In his well-known statement the Irish poet has said of his poetry : "It is myself that I remake" and Ezekiel, in his "Foreword" to *Sixty Poems*, wrote :

> There is in each (poem) a line or phrase, an idea or image, which helps me to maintain some sort of continuity in my life.[14]

The Yeatsian impact is traceable in *Sixty Poems* where several images used by him remind the reader of Yeats's imagery. In "The Stone," the image seems to have been borrowed from Yeats's "Easter 1916" — "The stone is in the midst of all." In Yeats's poem stone is the symbol of fixity that defies change. The image of the stone represents obsession of the Irish revolutionaries with the liberation of their country which in the process had rendered them heartless and inflexible. A parallel use of this image occurs in Ezekiel's poem :

> I have learnt to love the texture of a stone,
> Rough or smooth but all unyielding stone,
> Which plays no facile game of outward show,
> And holds itself together as a bone;
>
> (*CP*, p. 40)

The title of his fourth volume, *The Unfinished Man* is also taken from Yeats's poem "A Dialogue of Self and Soul" :

> The ignominy of boyhood; the distress
> Of boyhood changing into man;
> The unfinished man and his pain
> Brought face to face with his own clumsiness...
>
> (*CP*, p. 115)

Ezekiel believed in Yeats's dictum that poets, like women, "must labour to be beautiful," and the poem "Poet, Lover, Birdwatcher" (*CP*, p. 135) is a suitable case in point where the poet says "The best poets wait for words" like an ornithologist sitting in silence by the flowing river or like a lover waiting for his beloved till she "no longer waits but risks surrendering." Ezekiel, like Yeats, has managed to create his own Lake Isle of Innisfree : "He dreams of morning walks alone/And floating on a wave of sand" ("Urban", *CP*, 117). The only difference between them lies in Ezekiel's commitment to put up with "kindred clamour close at hand" instead of Yeats's "I shall arise, and go now, go to Innisfree."

T.S. Eliot's impact on the twentieth century poets has been so pervasive that no poet of substance could afford to remain uninfluenced by him. In his obituary on Eliot Ezekiel, refers to this phenomenon :

> Eliot's poetry from 1917 to 1943 is like the Himalayan mountains, with the Everest of *The Waste Land* several all but inaccessible peaks, a score or so of attractive but treacherous ranges (*A Song For Simeon*, *Marina*, *et al.*) and a miscellany of small, steep hills obscured in mist. *The Quartets* form a spacious, high plateau among the clouds. The air is rarefied but gracing, the winds are strong and chilly. The temptation to remain in this mountain-scape and to accept it as the only sovereign territory of poetry was irresistible to several generation of readers.[15]

Repudiating adverse comments on *The Waste Land* about its haphazard structural pattern, Ezekiel observes in the same essay :

> I think it is possible to make out a strong case for appreciating the poem despite its disorganisation, concentrating on its richness.... I consider it a great poem, not the oddity it is now widely considered to be. It is great because of the 'unity of a personality' expressed in it, which finally overcomes its disorganisation, once the requisite erudition is acquired by the reader to grasp that unity.

It should, however, not create the impression that Ezekiel is a blind imitator of Eliot because he also disagrees with him at times as in the following extract from the 'Obituary' :

> It is in fact painful to compare Eliot's liberating conception of the literary heritage with his constricting dogmas of the human heritage as a whole. Further the theory of how individual talent ought ideally to operate, and the vision of the existing monuments modified by the introduction

of a really new work of art among them, is so abstract and metaphysical that it adds little to our appreciation of specific masterpieces.

Eliot approaches the problem of human degeneration in *The Waste Land* in a typically Christian way — "I had not thought death had undone so many." Though not a religious poet, Ezekiel shares Eliot's diagnosis of human loneliness caused by a variety of factors. In poems like "Urban," "Island" and "A Morning Walk," Ezekiel vehemently denigrates selfish interests and material concerns. The denizens of Ezekiel's 'unreal city' of Bombay are no better than their counterparts in Baudelaire's Paris or Eliot's London in that they are simple human ghosts with nothing positive in life. Ezekiel's hybrid colonial city epitomises all the tensions and corruptions which had engulfed all the major European capitals after the First World War. In the face of a complete collapse of Western Culture — "London bridge is falling down falling down falling down" — Tirasias is at his wit's end —"Shall I at least set my lands in order?" — Ezekiel's protagonist "as a good native should" takes "calm and clamour in its stride" ("Island", *CP*, p. 182).

Ezekiel has been equally indebted to Ezra Pound, whose association with Yeats and Eliot is part of Modernism's history. He candidly admits that the American Imagist influenced him thematically as well as technically :

> The early influence on me of Pound and Eliot concerned poetry as an art, as well as on criticism of poetry, of society past and present, of modes of thinking and feeling, etc. But I never accepted the doctrines which Pound and Eliot, separately defined for themselves and their readers. I sorted them out for myself, modified them to suit my temperament, and so on. It would be misleading and unfair to say that Pound and Eliot influenced me only on the "technique side." Their influence was far reaching, even comprehensive, but I was never dominated by it. I used it and went back to it from time to time, noting how my growth changed my attitudes to their outstanding creative as well as critical writing.[16]

Ezekiel's poetry has an overwhelming impact of Movement poets like Philip Larkin and Donald Davie in its deft precision of phrase, common subject matter, self irony and allergy to hypocrisy. Larkin and his colleagues ensured that poetry ceased to be an instrument of propaganda, an official hymn as in the case of the Thirties poets, it must at the same time be saved from degenerating into romantic yearning of Dylan Thomas's variety. Ezekiel on his part had to keep at arm's length both, the romantic vagaries and also the misplaced patriotic strain of pre-Independence poetry. He has admitted his debt to Philip Larkin and this is most pronounced in his deliberate eschewal of intricate symbolism or far-fetched mythology, denigrated by the British poet as "common myth-kitty." David McCutchion has perceptively commented that Ezekiel

> belongs with Thom Gunn, R.S. Thomas, Elizabeth Jennings, Anthony Thwaite, and others like them. He has their cautions, discriminating style, precise and analytical, with its conscious rejection of the heroic and the passionate as also of the sentimental and cosy.[17]

The contention of Christopher Wiseman that the impact of the Movement poets was rather unhealthy for Ezekiel's poetic virtuosity, is not entirely off the mark. The Movement style did restrict Ezekiel's poetic canvas and his own real voice often got suppressed. To quote Wiseman :

> It is, I think, significant that Ezekiel never experimented with traditional forms to the extent that most British and American poets did, seeming to be content with strict accentual-syllabic patterns and relatively straightforward stanza-forms; and, for all his obvious innate talent, many of his earlier poems suffer from an almost mechanical rigidity, a monotony of sound which deadens and weighs down the bright buoyancy of his content.[18]

Enumerating his formative influences, Ezekiel wrote to Anisur Rahman that his poems written after 1965 have shaken all the influences howsoever dominant and irresistible they might have been in his early poetry :

> In the early stages, there were Eliot, Yeats and Pound, Rilke, modern American poetry from Whitman to William

> Carlos Williams, the poetry of the 30's in England, including specially Auden, Spender, MacNeice and Day Lewis. The later poetry is not under particular influence, because I had begun to resist them. All the poems in *The Unfinished Man* are obviously in the spirit of the Movement poets in England but from *The Exact Name* onwards, I am on my own again.[19]

The foregoing discussion shows that the development of Indian poetry in English received a pronounced impetus after 1857 with poets like Toru Dutt, Sri Aurobindo, Rabindranath Tagore and Sarojini Naidu. Their archaic, imitative and overtly Victorian poetic style was replaced by the post-Independence poets like Nissim Ezekiel, A.K. Ramanujan and Kamala Das with the introduction of contemporary idiom and intention in it. Ezekiel's Jewish marginality and exposure to European values turned out to be his great assets in transforming the existing poetic scene. Through his poetic formulations and creative parametres he embarked on his poetic journey and they will engage us in the chapter that follows.

REFERENCES

1. M.K. Naik, *A History of Indian English Literature* (New Delhi : Sahitya Akademi, 1982, rptd. 1995), p. 23.
2. K.R. Srinivasa Iyengar, *Indian Writing in English* (New Delhi : Sterling, 1962, rptd. 1990), p. 205.
3. Bruce King, *Modern Indian Poetry in English* (New Delhi : Oxford, 1987, rptd. 1992), p. 1.
4. Kamala Das, "An Introduction" in P. Lal, ed. *Modern Indian Poetry in English : An Anthology and Credo* (Calcutta : Writers Workshop, 1969), p. 104.
5. P. Lal and K. Raghavendra Rao, eds. *Modern Indo-Anglian Poetry* (Calcutta : Writers Workshop, 1958), p. 15.
6. Pritish Nandy, ed. *Indian Poetry in English Today* (New Delhi : Sterling, 1973), pp. 6-7.
7. Nissim Ezekiel, *Collected Poems* (Delhi : Oxford, 1989, rptd. 1994), p. 179. Hereafter referred to as *CP*.
8. Nissim Ezekiel, "An Interview with Nissim Ezekiel," *Selected Prose* (Delhi : Oxford, 1992), p. 163. Hereafter referred to as *Selected Prose*.
9. Eunice de Souza, "Interview with Four Indian English Poets" (1989), *The Bombay Review*, 1 (1989), 75.

10. R. Raj Rao, *Nissim Ezekiel : The Authorized Biography* (New Delhi : Viking Penguin, 2000), p. 60.
11. Susheel Kumar Sharma, "Fourteen Questions to Nissim Ezekiel" in T.R. Sharma, ed. *Essays on Nissim Ezekiel* (Meerut : Shalabh Prakashan, 1994), p. 42.
12. Suresh Kohli, "Nissim Ezekiel : An Interview," *Mahfil* (now *Journal of South Asian Literature*), 8, 4 (1972), 8.
13. Chetan Karnani, *Nissim Ezekiel* (New Delhi : Arnold Heinemann, 1974), p. 30.
14. Quoted in *ibid.*, p. 27.
15. Nissim Ezekiel, "Eliot's Language : Thirst and Fear," *Times of India*, 6 April 1989, 8.
16. S.K. Sharma, "Fourteen Questions to Nissim Ezekiel" in T.R. Sharma, ed. *Essays on Nissim Ezekiel, op. cit.*, p. 44.
17. David McCutchion, "Examen de Midi," *The Miscellany*, 29 (Oct. 1968), 71.
18. Christopher Wiseman, "The Development of Technique in the Poetry of Nissim Esekiel : From Formality to Informality," *Journal of South Asian Literature*, 11, 3-4, (Spring-Summer, 1976), 241.
19. Anisur Rahman, *Form and Value in the Poetry of Nissim Ezekiel* (New Delhi : Abhinav, 1981), p. 79.

2

Views on Poetry

In one of his major statements T.S. Eliot underlines the essential link between the critical and the creative writings of a poet :

> When the critics are themselves poets, it may be suspected that they have formed their critical statements with a view to justifying their poetic practice.[1]

Again in his essay "The Music of Poetry" written after a gap of some twentyfour years, Eliot reiterates that "the poet, at the back of his mind., if not as his ostensible purpose, is always trying to defend the kind of poetry he is writing or to formulate the kind that he wants to write."[2] He treated his literary criticism as "a by-product of my private poetry workshop" ("The Frontiers of Criticism"). Eliot's statement provides an insight into analysing Ezekiel's views on poetry which we propose to undertake in the following pages.

Although Ezekiel has not brought out any specific volume on literary theories, his views on poetry and poetic process lie scattered in his essays, book-reviews, interviews and poems and his poetic creed can be formulated by putting them together. At the time of Ezekiel's emergence, Indian poetry in English had a colonial character in that it was imitative of the late Victorian and the Georgian poetry. Suffused with romantic day-reaming it was highly mystical in character, inadequate to cope with contemporary sensibility. Ezekiel began with dislodging the great literary monuments like Sri Aurobindo and Sarojini Naidu who had been dominating the poetic scene indisputably. He finds Aurobindo's *magnum opus Savitri* "embarrassingly bad : dated in language, emotionally inflated to the point of grotesqueness and confused in idea.... In my opinion, anyone who thinks highly of Sri Aurobindo has no feeling for the English language."[3] His criticism of Aurobindo's views on poetry contained in *The Future Poetry* which he takes up further, is equally sharp for

> that peculiarly vapid and windy idiom which intoxicates many Indian students of English literature...vision becomes a substitute for logic and analysis. The experience of poetry is replaced by ideology, in this case that of evolutionary mysticism.

Ezekiel is milder in case of Sarojini Naidu :

> It was Sarojini's ill luck that she wrote at a time when English poetry had touched rock-bottom of sentimentality and technical poverty. By the time it recovered its health she had entered politics, abandoning the possibility of poetic development and maturity.[4]

It was against the existing scene of "Asiatic vague immensities," that Ezekiel attempted to introduce contemporary idiom in poetry. He vehemently argued for shunning the fruitless dialogue with eternity, long loud wails at the human predicament and a garrulous search for the spiritual to man's fate marked by empty platitudes and sterile pity. He laid all emphasis on an authenticity of experience that revealed the emotional reaction of the poet to the poignant conflicts between tradition and modernism, the rural and the urban, prevailing superstitions and scientific outlook. In his exhaustive commentaries on the propounders of the Modernist movement, Ezekiel dwelt at length highlighting their poetic virtuosities which could serve as poetic models. Admiring Eliot's expression of abstract ideas with the use of concrete images in "East Coker", he writes :

> The imagery...is of our time, how perfectly it suits the feeling being expressed, and how effective the technique is of moving from the abstract idea to the concrete particular and back again.[5]

Apparently with a view to underlining Aurobindo's limitations, he refers to W.B. Yeats whose concern for the fate of human race is beautifully manifested in "The Second Coming." Ezekiel demonstrates how Yeats transmutes even crude ideas into poetry by the magical touch of his imagination :

> When the traditional framework breaks down, when for instance Christianity in Europe or America no longer provides a natural source of belief, such a poet as W.B. Yeats creates his own framework. He turns to magic and mysticism for his poetic mythology, drawing symbols from these for enriching his meanings. Even when none of his ideas are acceptable to the reader, he does not find it difficult to concede that the ideas strengthen the poetry, that they illuminate patterns of experience with which he is familiar, that they make the texture of poetry more interesting.[6]

It shouldn't create the impression, however, that Ezekiel treats philosophy as inimical to poetry. He takes up this issue in his essay "Poetry and Philosophy"[7] : Praising the metaphysical poets for their inclination to philosophy while taking high flights on the 'viewless wings of Poesy', he writes :

> In their intellectual and analytical moments, they express a complex sensibility. They project moods which include ideas or even philosophy but the ideas and philosophy are swallowed up in the moods, in the final product which can only be called poetry....

This essay discusses the relationship between these two major disciplines — poetry and philosophy — and identifies their common concerns. He opines that a good poet should aim at infusing a certain amount of philosophy in his poems. Commenting on the poetry of John Donne and his contemporaries of the 17th century, Ezekiel further observes :

> If we squeeze out the philosophy from it (the metaphysical poetry) we shall obtain the verbal equivalent of dishwater, but within the poetry and an inseparable part of it, the philosophy is power or magic, it is the animating principle, the source of linguistic strength and beauty.

However, Ezekiel is conscious of the fact that too much of philosophical content mars the spirit of poetry. In absence of a balance between these two, the lyrical quality gets subverted and poetry ceases to be a source of communication because superficiality creaps in. To quote him :

> ... What happens when a poet is merely thinking and versifying his ideas is that the rhythm becomes loose and feeble, the language tends to be ordinary, the images are more like flowers in a vase than depth charges.

Philosophy; in this way, should be merely a part of poetry, the less the better, and not the whole of it. The reader would feel bored enough if thinking gets an upper hand :

> ...preoccupation with ideas may conceivably weaken that grasp of minute particulars which Blake recommended, that intimacy with the concrete and commitment to personal experience which the poet cultivates.

Ezekiel points out that a great thinker and intellectual giant may not necessarily be a good poet. Citing the case of Emerson he comments in the same essay that though a stimulating thinker, the American poet cannot be considered a great poet :

> It has often been said that he was essentially a poet, even in his thought. Unfortunately, though the poems are readable enough, they are rarely strong in rhythm and imagery. They do not tell us more of the man than we know from prose nor do they stand independent as admirable examples of poetic art. Our interest in them is almost entirely because they are Emerson's. We hear his voice in them.

Differentiating poetry from philosophy Ezekiel takes the former as the art of language while the latter is the play of thought. In poetry, the artful use of words is important while philosophy aims at the depth of thinking. In Ezekiel's words :

> The nourishment poetry provides to the soul is through the senses and the capacities of thinking and feeling are exercised by using words as signs and symbols, in addition to using them as meanings. That is why in poetry the sound and weight of words, their texture and associational values, their rhythmic relation to other words, and their special status in the language at a particular time as well as the new uses to which they can

> be put, is of highest importance. Poetry is an art of language, philosophy is an art of thought.

Ezekiel's views on poetic principles can be further traced in his "Poetry as Knowledge" where he tries to forge a relationship between poetry and knowledge. Here again he proclaims that just as philosophy, knowledge too has an important say in creation of good poetry. Stressing the significance of knowledge in poetry, Ezekiel says :

> Since poetry is, at the very least, a mode of human speech, it inevitably contributes to man's knowledge of himself and of the world in which he lives. It ought not to be considered in relation to metre, metaphor, image, symbol, structure, texture, tension and so on. These are the means of poetry, not its ends, which are meaning, knowledge, and truth. I place knowledge at the centre of the trinity. It is the source of strength for the other two.[8]

Ezekiel further adds that knowledge, at least, gives weight to the poetry and a poem shorn of knowledge is volatile. But this knowledge has to be expressed artfully and should appear alive : "...yet when we speak of poetry we ought to mean poetry as a particular mode of literary expression only. Otherwise, we shall soon arrive in the camp of the advertising copywriter who describes women's garments as poetic or a kitchen sink as lyrical." In Ezekiel's view, poetry has got to be different from pure knowledge or thought. Pure knowledge could well be the domain of philosophy and sciences, but certainly not this could be the sole aim of poetry. Poetry becomes frustrating if it is not experienced as poetry alone. Poetry and ideas must go side by side. The art of the poet is best appreciated only when ideas, howsoever abstract, are smoothly infused in the body of poetry — without the least obstruction in enjoying it.

Ezekiel, in his typically characteristic way, never presents a lopsided view of things and warns against the creation of poetry which surpasses its limits and lands up in the terrain of propaganda. Poetry must not be overloaded with the ideas or knowledge for the fear of its being merely a carrier of a particular 'ism'. He would loathe to think of such poetry :

> Versified knowledge is rightly denigrated, superfluous as knowledge and superficial as verse. Poetry as propaganda is equally suspect. The surrealist movement in poetry, claiming to arrive at a truth by using automatic modes of writing derived from the alleged workings of the unconscious, failed miserably to produce much poetry with staying power. Marxist poetry is more Marxist than poetry.... To be good, poetry has to be an independent art.

Ezekiel seems to voice the controversy between poetry as art and poetry as propaganda which reached a new height with later Modernists like W.H. Auden and his colleagues. He sounds anti-Caudwell in siding with Auden who diluted Modernism in his poetic practice particularly in his early years. Similarly, Ezekiel is a Modernist poet with a difference. While Eliot wanted poetry to be esoteric in nature since the poet had to communicate an unusual experience which could be comprehended only by a select few, Ezekiel wants poetry to be more accessible to the reading public :

> ... indifference to communication, if it becomes widespread, decreases the audience for poetry disastrously. This happened with certain poetic movements in our time. There were sound reasons for paying the price.... Fortunately, alternatives to the hermetic and scholarly style in poetry opened up as times changed. In fact later, a more accessible poetry was written in England and America and continues to be written.[9]

Later in the same essay, "Should Poetry be Read to Audiences?" Ezekiel addresses himself to other allied issues like language of poetry and the purpose of poetry. He is in favour of "bringing the poet into the centre of society, restoring to him his natural voice as seer and prophet, and establishing a more human relationship at the same time between him and his audience." Ezekiel pleads for transparency and simplicity in poetry towards the close of the essay :

> Attacks on obscurity in poetry are generally dismissed as anti-intellectualist. But there still remains a case against always giving obscurity and difficulty the benefit of the

> doubt on the ground that some profound truths can be expressed in no other way. Too many poets in the twentieth century offer only the difficulty and not the profundity, though it is not considered respectable in literary circles to be so. I take the risk of saying so.[10]

This argument in favour of simplicity, however, is not at the cost of profundity of thoughts which do demand uncommon ways of expression. As if to dispel any such misgivings Ezekiel writes in "Uncertain Certainties," Nov.-Dec. 1975 :

> The normal modes of communication do not work when certain kinds of insight (inspiration) are experienced. So a story is told, a symbolic situation devised, an aphorism formulated, a poetic sequence of sounds created or a paradox crystallised.[11]

The poet himself has employed a not-so-simple style in his "Poster Poems" which have a relatively serious content. He admits in a brochure for the third exhibition, "I chose to take the risks of complexity, compression and stylistic free-wheeling, particularly in the treatment of certain mystical or metaphysical perceptions." This suggestion for obliqueness, which is obviously different from obscurity, has its own logic behind it. An oblique presentation of a serious truth becomes more compelling and thought-provoking. Verbal clarity is not always a desirable proposition :

> But even the simplest idea has dimensions which verbal clarity distorts or altogether destroys. Many a clarified idea is an empty shell. It makes a clacking sound when put together with other empty shells.[12]

It is this conviction about his art which prompted Ezekiel to claim, "...even the most complex of my poems are relatively simple and direct, judged by the norms of difficult poetry properly so-called."[13]

Though a Modernist writer Ezekiel is a classicist in his poetic preoccupations like his mentor T.S. Eliot who declared himself to be a 'Classicist in literature, Anglo-Catholic in religion and Royalist in politics' in 1927. For Ezekiel, poetry is a conscious art — "Involvement in poetry, comprehensively, is of course the first condition." In his essay "To Revise or not to Revise" (*Selected*

Prose, pp. 20-28) he has deliberated on this problem at length. The very title recalls Pope's famous couplet :

> True ease in writing comes from art not chance,
> As those move easiest who have learnt to dance.

Stating his creed in unequivocal terms, Ezekiel says :

> If I had to state my personal credo on this theme, in the context of writing poetry, it would merely be : Revise or Be Damned.... To revise implies, at its simplest, to reconsider and be willing to improve.... What if revision makes worse instead of improving? Suppose reconsideration ends by watering down, compromising, obscuring instead of making more precise? (p. 20).

The poet is quick to warn, however, that this act of revision should not interfere with the idea of the poem :

> ... minor changes may be made, a few alterations here and there, but the essential steam flows as it does. To change its direction or to reduce its quantity is sacrilege. This is a slightly more reasonable stance, or seems to be, but the emphasis is still on the same belief or faith in inspired utterance (p. 21).

Ezekiel's views on the revision of a written piece and the necessary inspiration for it could be traced also in his famous poem "Poet, Lover, Birdwatcher" :

> The best poets wait for words.
> The hunt is not an exercise of will
> But patient love relaxing on a hill
> To note the movement of a timid wing;
> Until the one who knows that she is loved
> No longer waits but risks surrendering —
> In this the poet finds his moral proved,
> Who never spoke before his spirit moved.

(*CP*, p. 135)

There is an inextricable relationship between inspiration and revision which always go together. A wholly inspired poem cannot reach perfection or cannot be necessarily validated if it is not revised. Commenting on this aspect of poetic process Ezekiel writes :

> I've never relied entirely on inspiration but feel no need to discount it altogether. What else is it but an inspired poem which comes when one is totally unprepared for it? I hasten to add that an inspired poem in this sense is not necessarily a good poem. The inspiration is a technical fact but has little or no validating force. The trouble with poets who experience this kind of inspiration is : they find it very difficult to believe that inspired poems may be bad poems. I, on the contrary, have to check the opposite inclination of being so suspicious of inspiration that I will not allow it to 'dictate' a poem to me (pp. 22-23).

Revision for Ezekiel "means raising the uninspired sections after recognising them as uninspired, to the level of the inspired bits or cutting them out."

That Ezekiel is essentially a classicist is testified to also by an incidence which he narrates in this essay :

> It was in 1967 in Chicago, where I was his (Ramanujan's) guest, using part of the available time... to revise a batch of poems I had taken along. I was very pleased when Ramanujan picked up one of my poems...and said it was inspired. Immediately afterwards he shocked me by saying 'If you cut out the first nine lines and the last fourteen lines, this will be a good poem'. I stammered something to the effect that since the poem had only 35 lines in it, cutting out 23 would leave only 12. 'Yes,' he replied, 'but those 12 lines are the inspired ones. If you want it to be a longer poem, you can revise some or all of the other 23.' Eventually, I cut some and revised others, making it a poem of 19 lines... (pp. 23-24).

The very fact that Ezekiel allowed his poem to be scissored and fragmented at the advice of a much younger colleague, speaks of his sincere commitment to poetic art. He specifically warns that revision must not entertain obscurity at any cost, "In revising poems, poets should guard against the danger of adding complexity like a varnish or altering a structure for the sake of a more intricate rhythm, which may choke the meaning. A poem should never be revised to accommodate mannerisms but to eliminate such as have crept in. Clearly, then, revision is a double-edged weapon" (p. 26). The essay closes on a note which indirectly recommends Matthew Arnold's 'touchstone method' :

> It would of course be disastrous if the reaction were in favour of spontaneous poetry, free from any formal discipline, a purely arbitrary outflow that is never checked for the sake of art but allowed to continue in the name of emotion. I am reminded of one Indian-English poet who claims that she doesn't even read other poets any more because she doesn't want to be influenced by them. That way lies the death of poetry as an art (*SP*, p. 28).

Poetry is certainly not a 'spontaneous overflow of powerful feelings' for Ezekiel as he referred to the writing process of "Poster Poems", "My 'technique' was to write each poem first at some length and then to cut it drastically till only an image remains." He also rejects Pater's theory of Art for Art's sake in a catalogue note to "The Egoist's Prayers" :

> In searching for a suitable poetic form which could be used on posters, I arrived at a number of starting points, from Vedic hymns to American Indian songs and Zen fables. Their origin is not important to me now. What is important is the distance they have travelled from it. Poetry is rarely *sui generis*. To go forward it has to go back first.

Ezekiel has made significant observations on the significance of form in poetry from time to time. In a letter to Anisur Rahman, he says :

> I cannot think of poetry without at the same time thinking of its form. Both in reading and writing it, the form belongs to the spirit and substance of experience. To find the form inadequate is to question the inadequacy of poetry, to doubt its full authenticity and significance. Right from the beginning into its inchoate sources, form is as much the aim of the poet as meaning in all its modes.[14]

Thus, in his view, form is as inseparable from content as spirit from the body. Ezekiel believes in the dialectical unity of form and content. Giving an account of his poetic method, Ezekiel remarks :

> In writing a poem, I want to make or construct a pattern of meanings, attempting as I go along to ensure that the task is worth the energy. It is possible to miss the goal by working at the technical effects so hard that the weakness, banality or obscurity of the content is overlooked. One has to watch the equation, consider the balance of form in the poem.[15]

He is not opposed to using traditional forms in poetry because it is idiom which is of prime importance in poetic composition :

> To use a traditional form is not to be outdated or old-fashioned. It is the idiom that becomes outdated and not the form. I try to use the contemporary idiom in whatever form it comes at the time of writing.[16]

In a group discussion also on 'Modern Indian Poetry' with D.J. Enright and S.N. Ghosh, Ezekiel underlines the importance of contemporary diction : "You cannot write good poetry in language which is not alive."[17] He believes that the poet must be fully familiar with the nature of words, their contemporaneity, their semantic bearings, phonetic associations and inner potency. Enumerating the chief ingredients of a poem he remarks :

> Tone, vocabulary, diction, sound all need precision in a poem, if the form as a whole is to be strong and not an approximation of some casual sense of it in the poet.[18]

Ezekiel's concern for technical perfection is also manifested in his letter to D. Ramakrishna, 27 Nov. 1977 :

> Certainly any poet is better understood by insights into his technique... I work carefully to be appropriate, to maintain a tone, to prevent anomalies or incongruities.

Overwhelmingly preoccupied with the search for a right idiom in poetry, Ezekiel never employs an effete poetic diction and asserts the right of a poet to recreate language. In his reply to P. Lal's questionnaire, Ezekiel said in 1969 :

> I think it is true that a poet must have the right to change and recreate language, but it is not true that this cannot be done by foreigners. In my opinion, it is not essential that a good poet should change and recreate the language, but if he aspires to be a great poet, he is likely to attempt the task. A poet acquires the right to change and recreate language by arriving at the existing possibilities (Very few poets arrive at these limits).[19]

One can sense an implicit resistance in Ezekiel's assertion that even 'foreigners,' the peripheral, can exploit the possibilities of language, which includes English as well. It is altogether a different matter that this can be attempted only by great poets. Similar ideas were articulated by T.S. Eliot in his essay, "Eighteenth Century Poetry" :

> Sensibility alters from generation to generation in everybody, whether we will or no; but expression is only altered by a man of genius.[20]

Though Ezekiel nurses some reservations about Eliot's theory of impersonality in poetry, he does feel that a poet should subordinate his ideas and feelings to the spirit of his art. To quote him :

> Without necessarily accepting Eliot's impersonal view of poetry, which requires an absolute separation between the mind that suffers and the mind that creates. I believe in the validity of his subsequent formulation : 'What happens is a continual surrender of himself as he is at the moment to something which is more valuable.[21]

It is this conviction to eliminate possibilities of subjective expression that Ezekiel warns against treating perennial human weaknesses as sources of poetry :

> Vanity and ambition cannot be the source of good poetry, but they can of course be its themes, and they do contain such direct or indirect expressions of the poet's vanity and ambition as consciously or subconsciously remain in his character and personality.[22]

Ezekiel also disagrees with I.A. Richards who regards poetic truth as half or false truth and thereby treats scientific truth as the parameter :

> To describe the statements of poetry as pseudo-statements, which I.A. Richards does, is to devalue poetry, even if unintentionally, in relation to the statement of science, accepting the latter as providing the norm. The distinction between the two types of statements in terms of true and pseudo is deplorable because poetry is true or nothing, though its mode of approaching, grasping and expressing the truth may be different from that of science. Poetic truth is not pseudo truth if such a term is permissible.[23]

One might construe from the above citation that Ezekiel rates poetry highly among human disciplines but it is otherwise. A tenacious follower of W.H. Auden who remarked 'poetry can make nothing happen' after his shattering disillusionment with Marxist ideology, Ezekiel takes a very moderate view of poetry and quarrels with those holding contrary views :

> ... I need to add a reservation about all attempts by poets and others to claim the highest status for poetry among the arts and sciences or, if more modest, to suggest that it has the same value as they do... Such defences of poetry which are innumerable, I consider futile. They bolster up the ego of poets and of those who are professionally associated with poetry, but do little more.[24]

The foregoing discussion of Ezekiel's views on poetry reveals that he is not a literary theorist in the sense one looks upon Wordsworth or T.S. Eliot who aimed at founding their specific schools of poetry. As a critic, he lacks their dogmatism and orthodoxy in that he shuns extremity of views. A perceptive reader of Wordsworth's and Eliot's poetry knows that they compromised with their poetic principles in later years. As late as 1994, Ezekiel evaluated his situation taking into account the total gamut of his poetic creativity :

> I dislike to be described either as old-fashioned or modern. But if you like, call me traditional — in the sense I do like poetry to have some kind of form and system like metre and rhyme. One who writes good poetry within the confines of metre and rhyme will write as well in free verse too.[25]

The analysis of Ezekiel's poetry to be taken up in the three substantive chapters that follow is intended to correlate his poetic theory and practice, besides examining his claim of being traditional.

REFERENCES

1. T.S. Eliot, *The Use of Poetry and The Use of Criticism* (London : Faber, 1933), p. 29.
2. T.S. Eliot, *On Poetry and Poets* (London : Faber, 1957), p. 26.
3. "Sri Aurobindo on Poetry," *The Times of India*, Sunday, July 23, 1972, p. 9.
4. Quoted in Sisir Kumar Ghose, "Sarojini Naidu : Towards Revaluation," *Osmania Journal of English Studies*, Sarojini Naidu Special Number, p. 28.
5. "Ideas and Modern Poetry," *Indian Writers in Conference* (Bombay : The PEN All India Centre, 1964), p. 51.
6. *Ibid.*, p. 54.
7. "Poetry and Philosophy," *Selected Prose* (Delhi : OUP, 1992), pp. 41-49.
8. "Poetry as Knowledge," *Selected Prose, op. cit.*, pp. 39-40.
9. "Should Poetry be Read to Audiences?" in H.M. Prasad, ed. *Indian Poetry in English* (Aurangabad : Parimal, 1983), p. 26.
10. *Ibid.*, p. 28.
11. *Selected Prose, op. cit.*, p. 118.
12. *Ibid.*
13. In a letter to D. Ramakrishna, 27 Nov. 1977. Quoted in D. Ramakrishna, "Ezekiel's Credo," *Journal of Indian Writing in English*, 14, 2 (July, 1986), 12.
14. Anisur Rahman, *Form and Value in the Poetry of Nissim Ezekiel*, p. 9. From Ezekiel's letter to him.
15. *Ibid.*, p. 39.
16. *Quest*, 56 (March 1968), 103.
17. "Modern Indian Poetry : A Discussion," *The Miscellany*, 28 (Aug. 1968), 66.
18. Anisur Rahman, *Form and Value in the Poetry of Nissim Ezekiel*, p. 68.
19. P. Lal, *Modern Indian Poetry in English : An Anthology and Credo, op. cit.*, p. 169.
20. *T.S. Eliot : Selected Prose*, ed. John Hayward (Harmondsworth : Penguin Books, 1953), p. 154.
21. Nissim Ezekiel, "How a Poem is Written," *Selected Prose*, p. 15.
22. *Ibid.*, p. 14.

23. "Poetry as Knowledge," *Selected Prose*, p. 34.
24. *Ibid.*, pp. 31-32.
25. *Indian Express* (Kochi), 12 June 1994.

3

The Romantic Phase

The poetic career of Nissim Ezekiel spans a period of over half a century during which his creative sensibility unrolled itself eventually ensuring him a colossal stature as a man of letters. Given his versatility as a poet and also his inexhaustible technical resourcefulness, it is a stupendous proposition wrought with risky generalisations to trace the significant milestones of his expanding poetic sensibility in specific terms. However, an indepth study of his poetic *oeuvre* demonstrates that it can be analysed in three well-marked phases — The Romantic, The Realist, The Humanist — for the sake of convenience. The Romantic phase begins with the composition of his "Early Poems" in 1945 and ends in 1958 and includes *A Time to Change*, *Sixty Poems* and *The Third*. The middle phase can be called the Realist phase and covers a period of about eighteen years from 1959 to 1976. This is Ezekiel's richest phase in terms of poetic output as it saw the publication of *The Unfinished Man*, *The Exact Name* and *Hymns in Darkness*, and also for the appearance of his well known representative pieces like "Night of the Scorpion", "Background, Casually," "Island" and "Good bye Party for Miss Pushpa, T.S." His recent phase commencing since 1977 can be christened as the Humanist which includes the Sahitya Akademi award winning title *Latter-Day Psalms*. These three phases have been examined in three substantive chapters of the dissertation. His early phase, *viz*. The Romantic one, will keep us engaged in the pages that follow.

Ezekiel's first book of poems *A Time to Change* (1952) comprising poems written between October 1948 and February 1952 is dedicated to Ebrahim Alkazi and his wife Roshanara as a token of gratitude for all they did for his visit to England. Prior to the publication of this volume, Ezekiel had written some poems which could not be published separately and comprise his second book, *Sixty Poems* besides other poems written after his return to India (though it contains 65 poems). This collection is dedicated to Elizabeth, one of his basement-room girlfriends in London. His earliest poems are printed under the group "Early Poems" (1945-48) in *Collected Poems*. Since the present study intends to chart out Ezekiel's evolving poetic graph chronologically, these poems mark pregnant suggestiveness both thematically and stylistically. Howsoever juvenile, immature and imperfect as poetic composition these pieces might be, they give an insight into the poet's expanding sensibility. The poet seems to have published them to manifest the obsessive priorities dear to his heart from the very childhood. Comprising nine pieces this group of earliest poems in the *Collected Poems* formed part of the flatly titled *Sixty Poems* (1953) which is prefaced thus : "There is in each (poem) a line or phrase, an idea or image, which helps me to maintain some sort of continuity in my life." What Ezekiel terms as 'some sort of continuity' in his life is vindicated in the very titles of these poems which refer to the persistent and recurring motifs in Ezekiel's poetry.

"There is a frequent focusing on and preoccupation with pagan woman in my poetry," admitted Ezekiel in his letter to Anisur Rahman.[1] 'Pagan Woman' is symbolic of fleshy existence, sexual vibrancy and emotional entanglement. His "Early Poems" amply testify to the poet's confession in respect of the treatment of love and sex in his poetry. From early on, as the piece titled "The Recluse" shows, the poet's approach to love was different from that of the general human lot which craves for unbridled sexual indulgence driven by "the clouds of drum-emotion." Their "daring stream of common passion" has its own pitfalls and hazards. The very use of the definite article 'the' is not incidental and qualifies the quality of insularity in the protagonist. The connotations of the word 'Recluse' do have a sort of religious burden. Ezekiel's modest love "sanctifies the violence of desire," something distinct from the usual voluptuous thrill :

> This secretive and modest love
> Is best, raining peace

Into the troubled night.
Mellow in the melody of light
That keeps the darkness dark,
And sanctifies the violence of desire
Clasped with arm and breast and thigh.

(*CP*, p. 81)

In "Dualism" the poet evinces how the two individual selves of the lover and the beloved with a host of temperamental discrepancies play "hide and seek between our kisses." Their "separate landscape springs to flowers" despite genetic dissimilarities. Ezekiel's avowed fixation with the anatomy of human body references to which are so pronouncedly scattered throughout his poetry has its first appearance here :

The silent moments of our love
Pose questions to
The regions far beyond our eyes :
Strangeness of a strange love!
Beauty of a distant world!

(*CP*, p. 83)

The last line — "Beauty of a distant world" — is a genuine romantic drive. The questions posed to the invisible 'regions' lead us to the poem "Delighted by Love". While satiating their passions, lovers feel elevated and sanctified :

Delighted by love, these stripped
Bodies dared the Everest,
... ...
By rituals holy in the temple
Where life creates and is created,
All kinships here are consummated,
By thrust of lust
When all that burns in breasts or lips is sated.

(*CP*, p. 82)

The conviction that all relationships are crowned in conjugal bliss remarkably evidences the poet's attitude to love's indispensability. However, the piece rightly titled "Question" begins with the query :

Is this the way to happiness?
Prolonging kisses till the world
Of thought and deed is dim?

This total immersion in sex at the exclusion of "thought and deed" unequivocally reflects the protagonist's priorities :

This laughing love of ours alone
Is wise and will remain,
When all endeavour has been cooled
By Time and mated to defeat.

(*CP*, p. 82)

The anguish of living in 'Time' and urgency to transcend it has been impelling romantic writers from times immemorial and quite often like the protagonist here, they find consolation through earthly love in the initial stages of their development. Ezekiel, however, is quick to dispel the impression that he indulges himself in romantic fancy. In the piece "Invocation," he prays to God to bless him to discharge the roles of common lover of flesh and blood deeply grounded in realities around him :

Initiate this late
Immaturity
Into the simple roles of man and lover.

The phrase 'this late/Immaturity' apparently unconsciously used, points to Ezekiel's inherent prejudices against the fleshly business as a votary of a monotheistic creed. He implores the Almighty to serve as a beacon lest he might stray into the mazes of blind love :

(And be)
The rudder to my eyeless loves,
The woman's hand upon the brow
Of this
Creativity.
Be myself whom I seek.

(*CP*, p. 83)

This seeking after brings us to the poem "Report" which examines the nature of love and the quality of its possession. The impersonal title controls feeling and induces an analytical perspective which distances the reader from the subject. The poem reads like Ezekiel's song of experience with overt touches of mistaken outlook :

> Possession is not, as once
> I thought it was, an act
> Of love, it is only
> A substitute in dream and fact
> For the ignorant and lonely.
>
> (*CP*, p. 84)

The undying lust cannot be possessed because of its passionate upsurge, immense and bottomless. Sexual 'possession' is a dream and its reality is ignorance and loneliness :

> And those who love are not,
> As people think, happy
> Because they love, but nearly
> Sad because the sea
> Of passion is nothing precisely.
>
> (*CP*, p. 84)

Though not published as a separate volume, these early nine poems recall *Nine Experiments* (1928) by Sir Stephen Spender, Ezekiel's close friend during his short stint at the U.K. The senior British poet was hailed with the publication of his early poetry as "Shelley of 30's." No wonder these pieces herald the Romantic phase of Ezekiel's career rooted in the anguish, conflict and emotional turmoil of the evolving poet. Commenting on the Romantic strain in Ezekiel's early poetry, K.R.S. Iyengar perceptively writes :

> (in his first two volumes) He was painfully and poignantly aware of the flesh, its insistent urges, its stark ecstasies, its disturbing filiations with the mind.[2]

In fact, Ezekiel depicts nudity of human bodies in love vividly with disarming frankness, shorn of all inhibitions whatsoever. The poem "Lines" centres in corporeal analogy with basic thrust on contrasts of flesh and bone. The reference to the male sexual organ as "the hidden and oppressive bone," unusually hard and tough when erect and the resultant appeal to "Hear the throb of loins in love" has its own logic behind it :

Listen to the secret marrow,
Lung and liver speak the word,
Accept the long tormented breath
And tremble in the thick of love.

(*CP*, p. 43)

A context is created in which "hidden and oppressive bone... shallow breath...throb of loins...secret marrow...lung and liver" become symbolic of the nature of sexual love. Similar ideas form the crust of the sonnet "The Stone," where flux and flow, blood and flesh are equated with the superficialities of the outward show, in contrast with "hard, cold, heavy, shapeless, solid stone" which is brought into analogy with "the hidden bone". In this sonnet of two seven line stanzas, each line ends with the words flow or show, stone or bone; and this addition of repetition to rhyme lends the poem the structural solidity to support the theme :

I have learnt to love the texture of a stone
Rough or smooth but all unyielding stone,
Which plays no facile game of outward show,
And holds itself together as a bone;
It does not feel the paralysing flow
Of everything that is not hard as stone
But shares its nature like the hidden bone.

(*CP*, p. 40)

The phrase 'hidden bone' appears in about half a dozen poems of this phase and reflects the poet's corporal concerns. The protagonist of the poem "What Frightens Me" lays bare his personality as follows :

I saw it carnal in the arms of love
(Crushed, compromised and consummated).
I saw it making vows
With hidden weakness in the bone,
Unstable at nightfall and at noon.

(*CP*, p. 106)

"Situation" (*Sixty Poems*) demonstrates how women invariably indicate their advances by touching the parts of body close to penis apparently for sexual excitement. The poet narrates this experience in all innocence :

She tried her best to make me understand.
Her voice was intimately soft; one hand
From time to time caressed the air and made
Each point a confidence, *the other laid*
Unconsciously (*of course*) *upon my knee,*
Pressed home the facts I might have failed to see,
And caused her pure affection, nothing less,
Suggest a fine, romantic loneliness.
"You know precisely how I feel about it.
No other friend of mine remotely grasps it."

(italics mine, *CP*, p. 43)

The protagonist of the poem "For Her" appropriately enquires of his beloved :

How much of me you leave untouched,
And yet you touch me well.

He further elaborates what he means by "touching me well." The analogy of messenger and reply for evoking a befitting sexual response is marvellous :

The call of what you have not touched
Like some insistent messenger
Waits for a reply.

(*CP*, p. 67)

In another piece, the poet dwells on the peculiarity of earthly love with its total absorption in the chosen physical organs :

As lover, Love, you know that I am lost
In continents of thought, and every urge
To see, know, hear, touch and praise the earth
Is concentrated on your lips and thighs —
The strange mysterious way of earthly love.

("And God Revealed," *CP*, p. 25)

The nocturnal business has its own *modus operandi* exclusively confined to effective tools and instruments. The second sestina of the poem "Two Nights of Love" graphically depicts this pursuit :

After a night of love I returned to love,
The threshing thighs, the singing breasts,
Exhausted by the act, desiring it again

Within a freedom old as earth
And fresh as God's name, through all
The centuries of darkened loveliness.

(*CP*, p. 47)

Traversing the physical contours of the 'darkened loveliness' appear to be routine exercises for the poet so much so that he can never forget that landscape. The following stanza can aptly be cited here :

Ethereal beauties, may you always be
Dedicate to love and reckless shopping,
Your midriffs moist and your thighs unruly,
Breasts beneath the fabric slyly plopping.

("At the Party," *CP*, p. 98)

The advance from the above extract of the poem "At the Party" to the piece "At the Hotel" further evidences that it is the sexual mission which goads people to go to parties and hotels. The deliberate attempts to cover up their instinctive design, the participants visit such places on one excuse or the other. Ezekiel exposes this enterprize with utmost probity. The poem begins with "our motives were concealed but clear" and ends up with the same line. Visit to the hotel apparently to join some friends over a cup of coffee was prompted by the irresistible sensual urge to see the Cuban dancer naked :

On the dot she came and shook her breasts
all over us and dropped
the thin transparent skirt she wore.

(Italics mine, *CP*, p. 112)

Ezekiel habitually dwells on human anatomy while emphasizing the physicality of passion :

He wondered why his torso seemed
So unfamiliar and his thighs
As though they were not part of him.
Meagre was the flow of muscle
And the bone not bountiful
But all was soft and small and spare
And nothing quite his own but separate.

("Nakedness II," *CP*, p. 60)

Ezekiel's poem "Description" develops the single image of hair, secretly pronounced in thighs and inner parts of the body, in its multiple associations, overtly with erotic purposes. Written in free verse the piece is extremely sensual and borders almost on pornography in the phrase "between your thighs a wonder of hair", with its obvious reference to woman's vagina in all its paraphernalia :

> I will begin — but how should I begin?—
> with hair, your hair,
> remember hair,
> touched, smelt lying silent there
> upon your head, beneath your arms,
> and then between your thighs a wonder
> of hair, secret
> in light and in darkness
> bare, suffering with joy
> kisses light as air.

(*CP*, p. 48)

The poem closes on a note of guilt with the protagonist questioning his integrity as to his winding up the amorous transaction with the approaching dawn and the female partner unwillingly "binding up her hair." Ezekiel's early poetry abounds in erotic images with focal thrust on private parts of the body. The poem titled "The Female Image" portrays the woman persona lying "on the lonely pillow in the single room" exciting the "empty palaces" of the poet's fancy to join her. Given the rapacious appetite of the protagonist, the poet feels for a moment whether the exercise would be worth indulging in from the former's point of view :

> Shall her belly know the lust of Man?
> And shall he be contented? On his cheeks
> The hunger and the shame,
> While *the inner courtyards* of his youth
> Are beseiged (sic).

(Italics mine, *CP*, p. 68)

In underlining the essential 'lust of Man' the poet alludes to the inherent human debility handed down to posterity by Adam. The employment of martial imagery to encircle the confidential sectors of body produces mock-heroic effect. The poem evocatively closes with the following excerpt with the protagonist finally wishing her to adjust her body to his lustful operation :

> He will watch the virgin
> Wear his fever, wait or turn,
> Arrange her limbs as he desires,
> For so he sees the female image
> On the lonely pillow in the single room.
>
> ("The Female Image," *CP*, p. 68)

Equally evocative and emotionally stirring are the following lines from Ezekiel's "Love Song" :

> Beneath your dress I find you young,
> Rewarding to my explorations, certain,
> Soft and flowing,
> And tender to the touch of love.
>
> (*CP*, p. 74)

Confident of his success in his sexual odyssey, Ezekiel's protagonist never hesitates for a moment while Eliot's Prufrock in his "Love Song" fluctuates, procrastinates and ultimately remains indecisive and uncommitted. This congenital weakness for sex envelops even the deaf and the blind in its orbit not to speak of normal human beings. The poem "Declaration" aptly titled so, closes thus :

> Certain vases and women, however expensive,
> Fill the animal heart with wonder and warmth
> And deprivation is desolation
> ... ...
> Longing to be absorbed—
> No moral law can fill the void,
> Deaf and blind to all is appetite
>
> (*CP*, p. 94)

Fire is a traditional symbol of sexual lust which consumes human vitality. In his seminal poem *The Waste Land*, Eliot alludes to the moral bankruptcy of the European civilization in the wake of the First World War :

> Burning burning burning burning
> O Lord Thou pluckest me out

O Lord Thou pluckest
burning

(11. 308-311)

The text of the Fire Sermon of the Buddha can profitably be quoted in this context :

> All things, O priests are on fire...The eye, O priests, is on fire; forms are on fire; eye-consciousness is on fire, impressions received by the eye are on fire.... With the fire of passion, say I, with the fire of hatred, with the fire of infatuation; with birth, old age, death, sorrow, lamentation, misery, grief, and despair are they on fire.[3]

By employing associational devices in the poem "For Her" Ezekiel draws an analogy between burning wood and love. The controlling conceit in the piece is burning. The common human experience shows that burnt wood produces ash and smoke which may not be totally visible but its part disappearance can be scientifically accounted for. However, the fire burning in the lover's heart defies all 'incendiary' rules :

Love breaks the incendiary laws,
Blazing in a high wind
But staying good. The more you love
The less you burn away.

(*CP*, p. 88)

The wood is turned into ashes while love is eternal and lasting. The paradox underlines the quality of physical love.

In *The Waste Land* Eliot has used 'fire' as an ambivalent symbol, both for sensual passion and purification of fleshy sins. In his poem "Paean" Ezekiel endeavours ironically to lend it religious import though with a difference. Identifying specifically 'the geometry of love' the poet pleads that it is during the nocturnal amorous activities that the human body in all its naturalness and originality appears without any pretensions. Referring to the Christian ceremony of baptism the poem argues that the first induction into the religious fold is in 'fire' and not in water as the tradition would have us believe. The central word 'baptism' acquires a new dimension and imparts unusual significance to the piece. The poet seems to voice D.H. Lawrence's conviction that sex is sacred and a source of blessedness :

> Always the body knows its nakedness.
> The first baptism is not in water
> But in fire. The limbs are shaped to lock
> And love, the eyes — they say — show a strange light,
> And lives are welded which exist apart.
>
> (*CP*, p. 92)

As baptism confers Christianity, so does the experience of sex make a man real. This baptism in fire is the 'ritual of mortality' ever since The Fall :

> Wives or mistresses
> Put up their hair, restore
> The silk or rayon swiftly shed
> When kisses called the blood
> To act again the ritual of mortality,
> And variously remember....
>
> ("Night and Day," *CP*, p. 107)

In another poem titled "Admission" this 'call for blood to act' assumes greater significance and overt preference over mind :

> I am not sure of anything but this :
> The blood must leap before the spirit sings,
> Perpetual life is in the mutual kiss,
> Profusion only comes with patient wings.
>
> (*CP*, p. 90)

Here Ezekiel's discipleship of Lawrence, the apostle of the Dark god is patently pronounced, if one recalls the latter's well-known statement :

> My own religion is belief in the blood, the flesh as being wiser than the intellect, we can go wrong in our minds but what our blood feels and believes and says is always true.

In fact, Ezekiel feels that without body mind is incomplete and hence the indispensibility of the former to lend a semblance of perfection to man. The aphoristic conclusion of the piece "Nakedness II" is quite meaningful :

Then wanting to be the whole again
That this his body may belong to him
And let him understand, that in the working
Of his mind the body takes a hand.

(*CP*, p. 61)

Besides viewing the multiplication of 'the dying generations' as a product of passion, Ezekiel images even the poetic creation in terms of the metaphor of sexual activity. The piece "Creation" compares the production of a work of art to the birth of a baby. The required expertise can bring about cherished results in either :

The sunshine of a kiss can glow
Within a dozen poems, and a body yielding
On the summer grass, with *expert fingers*
Can release
A spring of words as fresh as women's eyes.

(Italics mine, *CP*, p. 79)

This discussion of creation brings us to the institution of marriage with traditional sanction for procreation of human species. Eliot's central concern was the moral turpitude of the inter-War-years, and his great admirer Ezekiel never treats of love as a bohemian activity free from social censor and religious sanctity. The piece titled "Marriage Poem" is a joyous and an exquisite lyric centring in conjual happiness. It focally thrusts on the need to make the marital love a blessing. It argues that the marriage enjoins upon the partners the quality of sacrificial love to render it lasting and cheerful. With the ebb of passion cracks inevitably the ecstasy of the present tense and earthly love is threatened to extinction. It is the attitude of mutual understanding and accommodation that can redeem the situation :

Earthly love, O earthly love,
Be active when you will
But let the quieter passion come
To every lover, till
The nuptial pattern is secure
Though you are still.

(*CP*, p. 46)

The use of the modifier 'quieter' as opposed to the fiery nature of physical love is very apt and telling.

The spirit of compromise calls for transparency and openness in behaviour and the protagonist in the poem "Prayer I" implores the deity for this strength :

> If I could pray, the gist of my
> Demanding would be simply this :
> Quietitude. The ordered mind.
> Erasure of the inner lie.
> And only love in every kiss.

(*CP*, p. 54)

The corrosive character of hypocrisy — 'the inner lie' — appears to be a distressing factor with the speaker and his wish for 'quietitude' is genuinely sought for. The mechanical everydayness bereft of honest feelings invariably sabotages the marital peace. The want of sincerity creates discord and the spouses cannot help questioning each other's uprightness and integrity. Beginning with petty quarrels this misunderstanding may lead to horrible consequences :

> At first the beloved merely finds fault,
> Later comes the slow unresponsive kiss.
> Between the first encounter and the friend,
> And the friend no more, the Truth is known.

("Sonnet," *CP*, p. 107)

The relationship built on distrust and duplicity not simply produces mental tension, it inevitably leads to emotional 'constraints of exceptional proportions also. The female persona in the poem "Situation" (*The Third*) "never spoke her mind" 'and the protagonist "looked beyond her eyes." This eccentric kinship — "She lied to be with him. He had his stock of lies" — fundamentally awaited despair galore. Instead of sorting out their differences they chose to live in reciprocal illusions. The end-stopped lines powerfully accentuate the sense of despair that gripped the unfortunate couple :

> They did not say a thing to counteract despair.
> Nor planned to satisfy the hunger in their eyes.

A little guiltily she smoothed down her hair,
And safe in her affection he told his moderate lies.

(*CP*, p. 109)

Hardly better is the lot of the spouses in "Episode" where the protagonist does feel but fails to express the salutary advice — "Forget our bonds and choose a common bond." The clash of personal preferences creates fissure in nuptial harmony. The use of the end-stopped lines in the following passages skilfully conveys the winding up of relationship :

Thus ended what was ill begun.
She lied to be with me.
I lied to myself
We sought romantic restfulness.
God sent three beggars.
We went back to our separate bonds.

(*CP*, p. 99)

Sometimes such petty quarrels ensue even over ignoble misadjustments as happens with the lovers in the piece titled "An Affair." The protagonist and his girl friend visit a movie and mark the lovers' kissing each other on the screen voluptuously. After coming home the female partner tries to imitate the celluloid sentiments in life which is not favourably responded to by the lover. Had they applied the slightest commonsense, the situation would have been saved from worsening the very moment, because life cannot imitate art because of its various compunctions :

And when she said : I love you, just like this
As I had seen the yellow blondes declare
Upon the screen, and even stroked my hair.
But hates me now because I did not kiss.

(*CP*, p. 11)

As a follower of a monotheistic religion — Judaism — Ezekiel shares with brethren of his religious creed the ingrained prejudice against the fair sex as the corruptor of flesh. The entire responsibility of the Fall is attributed to the Woman (Eve) traditionally in Christianity, Islam and Judaism. In poems like "The Old Abyss," and "For Love's Record" the poet articulates his animus against the female kind. The piece "Old Abyss" records the poem's disparaging comments about a girl and her alleged licentious conduct. One cannot unjustly search for the implied meaning of abysmal depth to which Man fell from Eden due to woman's seduction. The use of the verb 'torment' in the following excerpt with its physical and mental associations powerfully conveys the poet's perspective :

> This girl, once married, with a child,
> But now alone torments
> The men she knows
> With such magnificence in movement
> (I have died beholding it)
> They see the old abyss again—
> Desire with object near and far.

(*CP*, p. 48)

The past credentials of the girl who deserted her husband and child apparently due to her faithlessness present her as a voracious hunter prowling about new victims. The protagonist of "For Love's Record" shares identical impressions about the fair sex. The woman being talked about is known for gathering "men as shells and put them by," "such love as hers could bear no common code" because "She grew in love abandoning her ties." The use of the word 'sorceress' in the following lines with its evil associations attests to the poet's contemptible attitude towards womankind as if to keep his 'love's record' straight :

> With her I *kept my distance* (not too far)
> But heard the music of her quickened breath.
> Laughing sorceress to harlequins,
> Who gathered men as shells and put them by.

(Italics mine, *CP*, p. 110)

The poet's virulence against woman does not stop with the metaphor of 'sorceress' and he straightway ascribes witchery to her. The annoyance of the feminist writers with Ezekiel does not seem misplaced specially when we read the following lines where woman is presented as a devil spirit haunting man whether awakened or asleep. The redemption for man is possible only

> When the female animal no longer
> Haunts the bed in flesh or dream.

("Something to Pursue," *CP*, p. 18)

The animality best defined by living on the sensual plane imputed to woman who is on the look out for her innocent victim the man, hypnotised and helpless, is unfair to womankind even from the Neo-classical norms. No abuse can be more insulting than comparing a substantial section of humanity to animals and thereby ignoring their innate potentialities 'to regain the blissful seat of heaven.'

As if this debunking were not enough, the poet equates women to animate and inanimate creatures of the macrocosm thereby further reducing them to non-entity, not to speak of equality and evenness :

> That women, trees, tables, waves and birds,
> Buildings, stones, steamrollers,
> Cats and clocks
> Are here to be enjoyed
> ... ...
> The true business of living is seeing, touching, kissing
> The epic of walking in the street and loving on the bed.
>
> ("Conclusion," *CP*, pp. 96-97)

Though the poem argues for the acceptance of secular pleasure as a requisite for living and thereby integrating various human faculties, the bracketing of the fair sex with stones and buildings smacks of an inbuilt antipathy which can hardly be accounted for.

No Gentile or Jew worth the salt can overcome the sense of guilt and sin caused by involvement with flesh and Ezekiel is no exception. In the piece rightly titled "Penitence" the poet conveys through the symbols of 'wave' and 'sea,' the pressure exerted on him by the relentless urges of passions even though he is conscious of the 'muffled tumult' of sin and wishes to be penitent :

> I will be penitent,
> My heart, and crave
> No more the impulse
> Of a wave.
>
> But I am still a sea
> And hold within
> The muffled tumult
> Of a sin.
>
> (*CP*, p. 71)

The poet, however, discovers himself in a peculiar fix torn by the tension between powerful passions and an equally overriding sense of guilt. Though the 'labyrinthine' desires create a tormenting perception of culpability, the protagonist is simply helpless to subjugate them :

All the strain and stress of youth
Merely fire
Divided into thine and mine,
Or something less,
Desire Labyrinthine?
And all to win
The sour taste of sin?
Even so.
Let it go, let it go.

("Nocturne," *CP*, pp. 74-75)

Of Ezekiel's love poems, the piece "To a Certain Lady" (*A Time to Change*, *CP*, pp. 27-30) encapsulates all the joys and discords which weave the very texture of marital life. Written in conversational tone and divided in four parts it centres in the realization of marital love as a blessing. The opening division asserts the reality of the couple's love. The protagonist recalls the female persona's virginal coyness and offers his own definition of life within this new relationship. The poem begins on a sensuous note :

At first you hesitated, in your white blouse
And skirt of velvet, soft as hair,
But finally arrived in nakedness.

Notwithstanding the human fluidity and the insatiate character of physical love he invites his beloved to join him in celebrating the feast of life with the firm conviction that all these hurdles simply test their attachment to the physical world. The protagonist voices an authentic romantic urge in his craving for "the unknown and the strange"[4] :

Life can be kept alive
By contact with the unknown and the strange
A feeling for the mystery

Of man and woman joined exhaustion
At the act, desire for it again;...

In desiring for the sexual activity despite post-coital depressions the protagonist seems to falsify John Keats's apprehension of physical love in his famous "Ode on a Grecian Urn" :

All breathing human passion far above,
That leaves a heart high-sorrowful and cloy'd,
A burning forehead, and a parching tongue.

The second section reads like an epithalamion and has a very suggestive typographical arrangement. It draws a quietly beautiful picture of married happiness :

While the seasons
Come and go
Flow phoenix love
And constant be
While the turtle's
Voice is heard
For we are young
And we are wed,...

The last line — "And we are wed" — is pregnant with meaning despite its common content expressed in mono-syllables. Ezekiel feels that constancy of physical love is possible and permissible only in wedlock and thus dismisses free sexual entanglements.

With the third part, elements of discord begin. The employment of the telling image of leech eating into the vitals of domestic harmony is too striking to be overlooked :

Then, absences and quarrels, indifference
Sucking like a leech upon the flesh,
Crude acceptance of the need for one another,
Tasteless encounters in the dark daily
Companionship with neither love nor hate
By an image are redeemed,
By a mode of love expanding to a way of life,...

The male persona is well aware of the fact that intimacy and estrangement are parts of the conjugal game. They must evolve a sinewy strength to their relationship through a realistic understanding and cold acceptance of the human phenomenon.

With the fourth and final section, quarrel is introduced. The inventory of the lady's domestic items underlines her commitment to the external finesse rather than to emotional bondage. Interjections and choppy sentences express the protagonist's displeasure. As an experienced householder, he proposes to change the controversial issue thus :

> There's no need to sulk,
> Let's have some tea instead.

He is able to appeal to her good sense and finally the conflict gets resolved. Portraying man and woman as fellow voyagers, Ezekiel uses marine imagery to describe the human situation upon this planet :

> Launched at last, we have to tack our sails
> To suit the wind, respect the compass
> And the stars, the laws of navigation,
> Bind the freedom of our days
> To log-books and the ground work of routine,
> Signalling to Passers-by
> Who are on other routes but use a common code.

This struggle to achieve a helpless reconciliation prompts the poet to take recourse to a prayer for harmony with which the poem ends :

> Teach us, Love, above all things, fidelity to music,
> Sharpen our responses to the colours of creation,
> Lead us undeceptively to what comes after passion,
> And let us die, Love, as though we chose to, for a reason.

This petition to god of love leads us to the title piece of Ezekiel's first verse-volume *A Time to Change* published by Fortune Press, London in 1952. "A Time to Change" (*CP*, pp. 3-6) is a moral allegory that uses the journey and quest motif. It is a complex poem part lament and part prayer and the epigraph from the Bible and old Testament echoes like Book of Psalms or Prophets lends a moral resonance to the piece. Divided into five parts it traces the different stages of the protagonist's development with the perpetually growing recognition of his situation. The first section is devoted to his departure from home and the resultant apprehensions that await his journey. The persistent anguish to return to the inner centre bursts forth thus :

How shall we return?
Debtors to the whore of Love,
Corrupted by the things imagined
Through the winter nights, alone,
The flesh defiled by dreams of flesh
Rehearsed desire dead in spring,
How shall we return?

The protagonist does have a zest for life but feels handicapped due to the mind playing an upper hand in decision making. The following lines articulate his agony that mind and body are not in unison :

But when the mind determines everything
The leap is never made, the music
Never quite completed, redemption
Never fully won
From what has been, ...

This passage recalls to mind the significant extract from Eliot's *The Waste Land* where the poet admires the quality of commitment undiluted by prudence and intellect :

Datta : what have we given?
My friend, blood shaking my heart
The awful daring of a moment's surrender
Which an age of prudence can never retract
By this, and this only, we have existed....

(11. 401-05)

While identifying his weak spots the protagonist in Ezekiel's poem feels that "amputated gesture" and "incomplete absorption" or the product of his inability to confront his temperamental infirmity.

The second section deals with the protagonist's consequent desolation and the search for a new life. He regrets that the longing to reach the goal is thwarted by innate debility. Under such circumstances one should doggedly pursue one's ideal undeterred and undepressed :

Sly rust encrusts the aspiration,
Youth runs out of song

Until one learns to start again—
Love of life can always be renewed.

These lines suffused with an unusual gusto for life are marked by an impulsive romantic characteristic. One cannot help remembering the following beautiful excerpt from W.B. Yeats's poem "Lapis Lazuli" :

All things fall and are built again
And those that build them again are gay.

This determination to start the creative process anew prompts the protagonist to look into the desired pattern of future in the third section of the poem. The typical Ezekielian in him chalks out his programme thus :

To own a singing voice and a talking voice,
A bit of land, a woman and a child or two,

Accommodated to their needs and changing moods
And patiently to build a life with these;...

The most remarkable aspect of this programme is its mundane dimension of 'here and now'. He resolves to execute his ideal by drawing upon the advice from ancestors, friends and parents slightly altered to suit his purpose. However, his is not going to be an extremely selfish proposition and it must subsume the larger human interests in its ken :

And show his deep affection for the world
With words emerging from a contrite heart.

In the penultimate section, the protagonist devises means to reach his target. Despite being fully aware of human limitations he looks for 'right idiom' — "Precise communication of a thought" — and "Love reciprocated to a quiver." It is the dreams or the ideals which proffer incentive :

Subsidised by dreams alone
The stubborn workman breaks the stone, loosens
Soil, allows the seed to die in it, waits
Patiently for grapes or figs and even
Finds, on a lucky day, a metaphor
Leaping from the sod.

The final section recognises the need for penitential exposure of 'secret faults.' It resounds with the refrain "Secret faults concealed no more," which implies as if the protagonist had enough of concealment and avoidance of his frailties and wants to get rid of them. The image of the repentant sinner poignantly conveys his restlessness :

Perception in April
Of my condition
Secret faults concealed no more.
Withdrawn to look
At my condition
Secret faults concealed no more.

The poem closes on a typical human note, the ambition confined to "A bit of land/A woman too/ Grapes or figs/ And metaphors" and finally, and most importantly "Inside illumination" born of encounter with his personal self.

This self questioning, an irresistible romantic motif leads to the poem "Something to Pursue" (*CP*, pp. 14-20), specifically mentioned by the poet as a piece of personal crisis. In his interview with Suresh Kohli, Ezekiel admitted :

> Scores of my poems are obviously written for personal therapeutic purposes, but since you ask me to give examples, I shall mention "Something to Pursue" in *A Time to Change*, "A Morning Walk" in *The Unfinished Man* and "Perspective" in *The Exact Name.*[5]

Dedicated to the poet's brother Joe, the poem is divided into four parts preceded by Prelude and appended with Epilogue. As the title signifies, it centres in the identification of values, the poet must pursue as an artist. The tormenting yearning to overcome the tension caused by opposite pulls finds its expression in the opening paragraph :

High endeavour with intensities
Of feeling and of thought,
That I may see myself
No longer unresolved
But definite as morning,

Moving to fruition
When the season comes.

The first section vividly describes the persona's attraction for a life of simple pleasures and his desire for fulfilment through marital bliss. The following picture rich in romantic images is worth citing :

Out of doors, lightly clad on benches,
Easily amused in parks and places,
Full length in siestas by a river, roused
To crescendoes in sunshine or the long shadows
Of persistent summer days, pagan
Beside a girl or tasting freedom
On a bicycle,...

However, the introspective doubts begin to arise with the second section and the willingness to achieve perceptive clarity goads the protagonist to spot his share of human weaknesses :

Memory presents to him
An almanac of petty vices,
Dumb enterprises, modes of being
Vicious though respectable,
Or joyously in search of something new.

The hosts of petty vices irresistibly interrogate human commitment at each step and question if one is "Self-propelled upon a single track." The adherence to the singleness of purpose, in the face of numerous devices and formulas received from ancestry is not an easy task and the pursuer is destined to get distracted. The poet opines that in such a confusing predicament, one should follow the dictates of one's own conscience. Doing so might invite the ridicule of others but the quester should not be dissuaded :

And remember that the eagle
When he soars is always
alone.

This determination to outshine others by attaining eagle heights shows that singleness or aloneness is not always a negative virtue. Normalcy or commonness, reflected in conforming to traditional values is not necessarily an indispensible guide to creative pursuit.

An inescapable moral issue confronts the protagonist in the third section of the poem. It graphically portrays the sin of Christ's arrest by the crowd headed by his betrayer Judas in the garden of Gethsemane. Judas ultimately could not forgive himself for his treacherous act and committed suicide. His late realization of duplicity poses certain questions :

> Is sin supportable?
> Does commerce with it damn the soul?
> Is it the road to dissolution?
> Or must we know it first to reach the end
> Which may be beautitude, achieved by few?
> Or will it be the tragic view?

The section, however, closes without any clues as how to transmute this tragic situation into blessedness.

The final part addresses itself to the queries in three separate stanzas dealing with different stages of awareness. At first the protagonist surveys the reality around him and this can be christened 'insight-beyond-the-mask' stage :

> Facades reveal, the anger of loins
> Shapes the human face, the modest bearing
> Of a shy girl explodes in furious dreams.

The next 'knowledge-through-experience' stage begins thus :

> At the second stage I touched and listened
> With my finger-tips the breasts of harlots,
> The swollen belly of the fool,
> Loins of the poet,
> Hearts of businessmen,
> Princes' eyes.

The third and final stage of 'commitment-to-act' however, does not obliterate "my night of love" and also the situations enjoining upon him to set on the journey of personal quest.

Ezekiel defines his ideal in still preciser terms in the opening poem of his second volume *Sixty Poems*, titled "A Poem of Dedication" which reads almost like a manifesto :

> Not to seek release but resolution,
> Not to hanker for a wide, god-like range

Of thought, nor the matador's dexterity.
I do not want the yogi's concentration,
I do not want the perfect charity
Of saints nor the tyrant's endless power...

(*CP*, p. 40)

The above extract marked by the abundance of negative words, one each in every line demonstrates that the poet has deliberated exhaustively on the possibilities and the avenues available to him. The prescriptive tone betrays a transparent mind free from doubts and suspicions concertedly determined to go his ways howsoever insular, eccentric or whimsical they might appear to others. The incessant craze to resolve the conflict, however, cannot compel him to withdraw from his surroundings because he wants to grapple with all odds on his own terms. He announces that his is going to be a very modest and humble approach lacking in both the burden of 'god-like range of thought' and 'the matador's dexterity.' One cannot unreasonably find Ezekiel rejecting both Eliot's religious solution to the European crisis during the inter-War years and also the Machiavellian-Marxist remedy so vociferously propounded by Auden and his colleagues. Interestingly enough, Eliot and Auden were dominant technical influences on Ezekiel's sensibility. The poet further explains in the poem that his loneliness or insularity has got nothing to do with the similar activities practised by a saint or a dictator. 'Yogi' and 'tyrant' symbolise the extremity of values. Both reject the society but while the former knows his isolation, the latter is hardly aware of it. The poet knows that perfection is not a human quality and as such he is determined not to be a human like the yogi or inhuman like the tyrant. The poem stresses the need for a poetic culture of a sympathetic brand with the humanity around :

I want a human balance humanly
Acquired, fruitful in the common hour.

(*CP*, p. 40)

The sense of involvement with humanity is planned to achieve through ordinary means without resorting to superhuman or subhuman distortions. He reiterates his commitment to human betterment in the poem "Prayer II" :

Let me not be isolated
Uninvolved in Man's defeat,
But know my love reciprocated
Dancing in neutral street.

(*CP*, p. 56)

Nissim Ezekiel is a romantic poet with a difference and his romantic flights are not usually enthusiastic at that. The plea for total understanding between emotion and reason — "Broken by excesses or by/Lack of them" — has been suggested through a homely image which implies that such engineering should never be calculated or contrived :

Let reason and emotion fare
As man and wife; let them quarrel,
Make love or live occasionally
Apart, and then be reconciled,
But let them not, indifferently,
Empty the house of words and music,
Partners of a marriage in decay.

(*CP*, p. 12)

The avowed obligation to a temperate way of life striking a balance "Between the elan of desire/And the rational faculties" surfaces in quite a few poems of this phase and evidences his down-to-earth outlook to human situation. To cite a random example :

My lips lack prophesy
My tongue speaketh no great matters
The words of the wise are wasted on me
Fugitive am I and far from home
A vagabond and every part of me is withered.

("Lamentation," *CP*, p. 72)

Ezekiel's quest for self is closely linked with his love for nature and a substantial bulk of his poetry reflects his response to the external reality of the macrocosm. The need to identify and merge with the elements of nature is irresistible for him because it is a prerequisite for fruitful living. He is inspired by nature in its complex variety reflected in hill, river, sea, wind, rain, spring, birds and animals. Quite often the elements of nature in his poetry acquire a symbolic significance loaded with ethical values :

There is a landscape certainly, the sea
Among its broad realities, attracts
Because it is a symbol of the free
Demoniac life within,
Hardly suggested by the surface facts,
And rivers what a man can hope to win
By simple flowing, learning how to flow,
And trees imply an obvious need of roots,
Besides that all organic growth is slow.

(*CP*, p. 39)

Bewitched by the natural affluence of spring the poet attributes human qualities to it and desires to absorb its freshness and loveliness in his poetry :

Your prodigality of love
Will live upon my waiting page.
Freshness of the first spring green
On turf unnoticed, wash my words.
Let something sprout, let colour be,
Let gestures flaunt like banners,
And like flowers let them wear perfection
Both at the centre and in every petal.

("Song for Spring," *CP*, pp. 57-58)

Spring recalls to the poet's mind the first feeling of sex urge in the poem "Remember and Forget" which opens with a graphic description of the season's advent announced by the chirping of birds in "moderate warmth and cold" of April :

Remember now
The first vibration in the conscious blood.
The swift rising of the flesh above
The stream of habit, like a water-bird
Responding to a call upon the air.

(*CP*, p. 61)

In the piece "Song" he looks upon the green blossoms of summer as symbolising prosperity, charity and lucidity :

Summer blossoms on a tree
I gave myself prosperity—

Charity, lucidity—
Remarking in the mood of seems
The doom of all my traffic dreams.

(*CP*, p. 42)

Water in the form of rain is a traditional symbol of life and Ezekiel describes the renewal of life in nature under the magic spell of rains :

And so I went, as the weather cleared,
Walking on the wet road, to know
If the scene had taken on a novel glow,
Lamplight, moonlight, dripping branches, wet road
Purer, sweeter. And now I know,
It is just so.

("After Rain," *CP*, p. 63)

If for Wordsworth

One impulse from vernal wood
May teach you more of man
of moral evil and of good
Than all the sages can.

Ezekiel fails to "find a word for the wind." Puzzled by the all enveloping and pervasive nature of wind, the poet takes recourse to metonymy to narrate his comprehension :

Another word, a phrase full of it
Like a sail, verses
Moving smoothly like the wind
Over grass, on among the trees
Rustling down the leaves of meaning,
Sound evoking sense, a sudden
Heavy thud of fruit
And long silences
Over and under the surface of the wind.

("A Word for the Wind," *CP*, p. 21)

"Occupation" marks out the cumulative impact of rain and wind and creates a supernatural atmosphere summoning up Coleridge's "Ancient Mariner" :

It was a stormy scene;
Thunder, lightning,

A multitude of ghosts among the trees,
Darkness, cold and restlessness,
A screeching owl, bats,
Many strange voices,...

(*CP*, p. 24)

Besides owls and bats, crow is an ominous bird, usually treated as an oracle of grief and gloominess in Western tradition. In his crow-poems, Ted Hughes attributes them god-like power by creating his own myth, a kind of black Genesis. For him it symbolises amoral energy which persistently questions God's purpose and capacity. Crow is one of the most widely distributed birds, most omnivorous, largest and least musical of song birds. The following lines from Hughes's "The Black Beast" can profitably be quoted here :

Crow shouted after midnight, pounding the wall with a last.
Where is the Black Beast?
Crow split his enemy's skull to the pineal gland.
Where is the Black Beast?
Crow crucified a frog under a microscope, he peered into the brain of a dog fish.[6]

The arrest of Christ leading to His Crucifixion was engineered in connivance with Judas and it materialised with the caw of the crow. Ezekiel refers to this event in the poem "Something to Pursue" discussed earlier — "At the third denial when the cock crew/ Peter wept" (*CP*, p. 18). In "The Crows" written as "A Comment on Rimbaud's *Les Corbeaux,*" the poet records his disgust and displeasure at the "cry of doom" of this "funereal bird" :

I hear them from my narrow bed,
I do not love, I only fear
Their cries of hidden duty's word,
Unwelcome, loud, funereal bird.

(*CP*, p. 41)

Ezekiel, however, is not blind to the loveliness and charm of other birds which inspire man to live with renewed zest and joy. In "Sparrows", the very sight of the bird collecting grass and leaves for building its nest reminds him of the "Primeval root of all the rest" — "the mating and the nest" :

You may not doubt their single aim,
Which is to fly and then to mate,
Aroused to build with twig and leaf,
A nest sufficient for the need—
Open warm, and planned to give
A truly bird's-eye view of things.

(*CP*, p. 103)

Ezekiel's "The Behaviour of Love Birds" reflects his interest in ornithology and natural history. The behaviour of birds suggests startling similarities with that of human beings in their amorous games :

The more the female fluffs
the readier she is,
and the more the male is encouraged,
Finally, she solicits copulation
by leaning forward,
raising her head,
and her tail.

Newly formed pairs
are rather awkward.
The males make many mistakes,
are frequently threatened
and thwarted
by their mates.[7]

The lustful trials faced by the male birds in their mating with female counterparts allegorise identical ordeals to which men are subjected in their courtship with the fair sex.

Though titled "Aside," the piece, tells quite vocally that the sex urge renders even animals restless and they are equally impulsively drawn to it as human beings and birds do :

One cannot imagine
Elephants making love,
But it seems they do.
So also tortoises
And snails,
Or even other men

With women doing
What it seems they do.

(*CP*, p. 93)

"Insectlore" recalls the third stanza of John Keats's celebrated ode "To Autumn" where the great Romantic poet finds solace in the music of microscopic insects because the melody of nightingale of spring is out of question. Here Ezekiel concentrates on the life-style of these creatures :

Worm, moth, serpent, toad,
Gleaming in the sun
Or slimy in mud,
Helpless round a flame
Or as the joys of love
Fragile in evening air,
Tame the wanton tongue
With flash of wonderment,...

(*CP*, p. 102)

"The Worm" transcribes Ezekiel's admiration for life lived on animal plane, the life of impulse which lends "astounding strength to the otherwise ignoble creatures. The straight movement of the worm "directed/By an inner eye" reminds one of the following excerpt from Eliot's "The Love-Song of J. Alfred Prufrock," where the protagonist wishes for the concentration and singleness of purpose which helps the small sea creature pounce upon its victim and devour it straightway :

I should have been a pair of ragged claws
Scuttling across the floors of silent seas.

Out of envy to the unswerving strategy of the insect as opposed to his "absurd and devious routes", Ezekiel's protagonist kills it :

Then, in bitterness, I crushed the worm,
Sadly determined not to honour more
Its easy mocking victory. So now
It's dead. Pretty worm, where is your strength?

(*CP*, p. 10)

The closing lines — "Only in anger can I emulate/The worm's directness. I've killed the worm" — echo the self-castigating stance of the incapacitated modern man and his tragedy born out of his alienation from nature.

Of the natural Flora and Fauna that have arrested Ezekiel's attention, the small but swift animal squirrel arouses exceptional response in the poet's mind. Its agile activity suggests to the poet the metaphor of thought flashing in mind :

> But he must come,
> Fluent shape of him, to be caressed —
> As thought should be
> By definition of the mind —
> As to a home
> At any cost
> Bound.
>
> (*CP*, p. 62)

In his well-known poem "The Thought Fox," Ted Hughes also compares the swiftness of mind's movement to the quick paces of fox, another fast moving animal. This discussion of animal-poem will not be complete without reference to the two pet creatures, *viz.*, cat and dog. The piece titled "The Cur" records the poet's reaction to the sight of a bad-tempered dog of mongrel breed. "Gangrenous in a vital limb" and "drawn by some disorder of the brain/To fowl decaying stuff," the dog has nothing friendly and endearing about it and the poet's disgust at its sight has been conveyed through telling modifiers. However, instinctively a lover of all that comprises macrocosm, the poet is gripped by a sense of guilt in the closing stanza and forced to realize its creatureliness :

> 'I too am life',
> The image seems to say,
> 'Air, earth, fire, water,
> Joie de vivre — remember me
> As you remember breasts
> Held with lingering hands
> Or speech in quiet places.'
>
> (*CP*, p. 95)

In his poem on the domestic animal cat, the poet introduces the personal touch by using the possessive modifier in the title "My Cat." Underscoring its uniqueness the poet begins the piece by contradistinguishing it from Verlaine's diabolic cat and Baudelaire's Sphinx-like creature. He never feels tired of enumerating its homely qualities including its aversion "to relish milk" and also its unwillingness to devour the stored fish. Her disinclination to catch even rats most distinguishes it from other members of its community. The poem ends on a personal touch with the poet lovingly recalling its sovereignty in his apartment :

> She does not condescend to chase a rat
> Or play with balls of wool or show her claws
> To teasing guests, but in my basement flat
> Defies all animal and human laws
> Of love and hate.
>   One night I'll drown this cat.
>
> (*CP*, p. 66)

This extract calls up in its warmth the unusual incident associated with Sir Issac Newton's dog Diamond which, while playing in a natural way during its master's absence, once accidently tripped over a burning candle and set ablaze invaluable research papers strewn around. Ezekiel's cat in defying "all animal and human laws" resembles the great scientist's dog. While Newton on sighting the disaster hugged the pet crying out "Oh Diamond, little dost thou know the great damage thou hast done," Ezekiel expresses his joy and affection by pretending to be unhappy over the reign of chaos let loose by the favourite cat.

The desire to recapture and relive the childhood days is an impelling romantic urge and in his seminal work *The Prelude* Wordsworth wishfully recalls his adolescence and the full-blooded involvement in the French Revolution :

> Bliss was it in that dawn to be alive,
> But to be young was the very heaven.

Though Ezekiel lacks the British poet's political conviction and commitment, he ardently aspires to relive his childhood days just for their innocence, intact as they were from "adult anger" in the poem "The Child" :

> Once I was a child
> And knew the certain joy of mud and toys,
> The destiny of fairy princes, magic birds

And happy giants in the golden books
Whose colours sang the wonders I was born into.

(*CP*, p. 57)

The employment of the words with heavily loaded romantic associations — 'joy of mud,' 'fairy princes,' 'magic birds,' 'happy giants' — creates an aura of strange surroundings.

The foregoing examination of Ezekiel's poetry from *A Time to Change* to *The Third* shows the various facets of romantic strain in his poetic personality. The love poems betray a youthful and spirited response to the emotional upsurge of adolescence. Marked by disarming frankness, these pieces centre in mundane celebrations of sex punctuated with overwhelming voluptuousness. It should not, however, create the impression that Ezekiel romanticises love as if it were a business of some imaginary land away from 'the weariness, the fever and the fret'. In quite a few poems, like "Marriage Poem," "Episode," "An Affair" and "To a Certain Lady," he does not rule out the possibility of discord and dissension in amorous game unless the lovers develop mutual understanding and reciprocal appreciation for each other's feelings. In a handful of poems like "The Old Abyss" and "For Love's Record" he voices the monotheistic prejudice against the fair sex as the defiler of flesh which culminated in the loss of Eden. Identification with self and an abiding and persistent query as to its true identity has engaged the attention of the evolving poet in several pieces. The most salient feature of his quest for self is the realization of the dilemma and an impatient urge to resolve it as in the piece titled "A Poem of Dedication". The objects of macrocosm and the elements of nature do provide him thrilling sensations and the poet wishes to enjoy their embrace and serenity as in "Song for Spring" and "Insectlore." A discerning reader, however, notices the missing Wordsworthian spontaneity and impulsiveness which characterize poems like "The Daffodils," "To the Cuckoo" and "The Rainbow." The rustic ambience and primitive innocence best typifies Romantic poetry and its absence in Ezekiel can be attributed to his urban upbringing and metropolitan ethos. The last piece of this phase "December '58" (*The Third*) evidences that the poet is looking for "an unflawed page" henceforward and "The night is now a distant show." With the passing of the year 1958 he visualises a new future with well-defined concerns and commitments :

> I must define myself, the place
> And time, the starting line or tape,
> To mirror for the seeking face
> What love of self distorts its shape.
>
> (*CP*, p. 112)

This resolution to relate himself to his environment and surroundings in terms of place and time, is powerfully executed in the second phase of his poetic career which forms the content of the next chapter.

REFERENCES

1. Anisur Rahman, *Form and Value in the Poetry of Nissim Ezekiel, op. cit.*, p. 43.
2. *Indian Writing in English* (New Delhi : Sterling, 1962, rptd. 1990), p. 657.
3. Henry Clarke Warren (select. & trans.), *Buddhism in Translation* (Cambridge, Mass. : Harvard University Press, 1953), pp. 351-53.
4. See Walter Hortio Pater's well-known definition of Romanticism as "Strangeness added to beauty."
5. *Mahfil* (now *Journal of South Asian Literature*), 8, 4 (1972), 9.
6. Ted Hughes, *Selected Poems* (London : Faber, 1982, rptd. 1984), p. 119.
7. Quoted in Chetan Karnani, *Nissim Esekiel, op. cit.*, p. 48.

4

The Realist Phase

The middle phase of Ezekiel's poetic development covers the years between the publication of *The Unfinished Man* (1959) and *Hymns in Darkness* (1976). As noted in the preceding chapter, Ezekiel's quest for defining self acquired a new dimension with the firm resolve to relate himself to two things, the place and the time. With this his art achieves a touching poignancy grounded as he is in a locale, the city of Bombay which becomes a central metaphor, an invisible presence in his poetic universe. Closely allied to this proposition is the poet's realisation of his relevance only to modern India. The quality of self-effacement, the urgency of casting off Narcissism to ensure a convincing self-appraisal and the import of employing critical attitude even in relation to native ethos had been isolated as trusted determinants to overcome the whole gamut of personal crisis. Unlike the early juvenile years when the poet's romantic fancies soared in distant unknown lands, one finds him now attracted towards the realities around himself. The process of executing the earlier resolution to define himself in terms of time and place had obviously started but the usual preoccupations are intermittently discernible in quite a few poems.

The Unfinished Man is a collection of poems written in this transitory period with deep imprints of personal questioning of values occasioned by a sudden exposure to a peculiar ethos, neither confronted nor envisaged so far. It looks back to one of Ezekiel's early pieces "First Theme and Variations" (a prose poem in *The Third*, *CP*, pp. 75-76) for its title. The relevant portion can be profitably reproduced here :

> I know a man whose definition in a word is chaos, but listened to his cry because he strove *to be a finished man*. I found him haunted by a passion for the truth about himself; he had been long in abandoning the urge to be loved and understood.
>
> (italics mine, *CP*, p. 75)

The endeavour to be "a finished man" and the restlessness to identify his true self — as "a passion for the truth about himself" — form the crust of this volume rightly titled *The Unfinished Man*. All the ten poems comprising the volume were written in a single year 1959 in the office and factory of Chemould where Ezekiel worked as General Manager. All the pieces are epistemological in character and form a sequence concerning the discontents of an apparently settled life, and are, as such, related more by theme than by story. They record a period of personal purgatory concluding with the possibility of redemption. The volume moves from generalization towards the personal, from complaint to decision and the ideal. David McCutchion[1] perceptively treated the book as "examen de midi" (an examination of one's life in the middle of its course). It is altogether a different matter that Ezekiel's predilections to identify his self in one form or the other continue till date, much beyond the biblical span of three score and ten which he has happily beaten.

The epigraph borrowed from W.B. Yeats's "A Dialogue of Self and Soul" (*The Winding Stairs and Other Poems*, 1933) focuses on "the toil of growing up," the impelling urge to outgrow adolescent proclivity into the sagacity of manhood, to inevitably end up in the process of becoming, never being. Given his inherent disorderliness man has to groan and grouse as the following excerpt from the epigraph demonstrates :

> The ignominy of boyhood; the distress
> Of boyhood changing into man;
> The unfinished man and his pain
> Brought face to face with his own clumsiness....
>
> (*CP*, p. 115)

The opening piece "Urban" grapples with the inner struggle of the city-dweller sandwiched between the pull of 'the city and the desire to escape its aimless clamour. Although it uses the third-person method of narration, the poet himself is the protagonist. The first stanza underlines the mechanical movement and habitual actions of the protagonist leading a routined existence. It abounds in archetypal life symbols — hills, rivers, winds. Hills symbolize vision, unity and perfection and as the ill-luck would have it they are far beyond his approach. The confrontation between two sets of values — urban chaos and imaginary quietitude — is the content of the second stanza. Completely ignorant of the natural phenomena, the protagonist neither marks the beauty of the morning sky nor feels the mystery of the approaching night. 'Dawn' and 'night' symbolize the principles of light and darkness while sun and rain are generative symbols of light and life in the cosmos. His is in fact an empty and meaningless existence — "He welcomes neither sun nor rain./His landscape has no depth or height." The unusual conglomeration of negatives conveys the quality of persona's entity. Both the first and the last lines of the stanza reveal the setting to be a not-too-tall building. One recalls that Readymoney Mansion or Mazda Mansion where Ezekiel lived was a relatively small building complex from where he could see neither the sky, nor experience a sense of depth or height.

The final paragraph draws a precise picture of his surroundings and also of the options open to him :

> The city like a passion burns.
> He dreams of morning walks, alone,
> And floating on a wave of sand.
> But still his mind its traffic turns
> Away from beach and tree and stone
> To kindred clamour close at hand.

(*CP*, p. 117)

The analogy drawn between city and passion — between something concrete and abstract — is a typical Modernist device imitated after the German poet Rilke to communicate a startling experience. The instinctive mindset for "a kindred clamour close at hand" foils all dreams of morning walks and their attendant joys. The allusions to 'beach,' 'tree' and 'stone' represent three cherished realms of human involvement. 'Beech' recalls Ulysses's enchanted love with sea creatures while 'tree' stands for natural flora. 'Stone' in the form of temple is a living embodiment of communal life, an archetypal symbol of community existence. The urban protagonist's alienation from love, nature and religion spells his doom which he cannot voluntarily avoid. The employment of alliterative device is intentional rather than incidental. The 'k' sound in 'kindred,' 'clamour', 'close' intones a defunctive music and communicates the raucousness of the city life and its tiresome pattern of living.

The persona's 'dreams' of morning walks bring one to the poem titled "A Morning Walk," incidentally the second piece of personal anguish mentioned by Ezekiel in his Kohli interview. This is the first exhaustive and elaborate picture of the city of Bombay. The poem opens with the poet revealing the persona's inner turmoil and utter confusion at the sordid state of his affairs. The city appears to him to be transformed into a symbol of decomposed garbage "Where only human hands sell cheap". This has been a persistently recurring phenomenon with him and his attempts at inculcating genuine love for the elements of nature could utmost make "his blood a sluggish stream". The rampant squalor and chaos has been conveyed by the image of 'marsh' and the poignant irony in the line — "His native place he could not shun" — suggests that the avenues for him are pitiably restricted. The sense of nagging adjustment to an unredeemable plight in jeopardy is too pronounced to be missed.

The protagonist's anguish explodes in the third stanza in a typical Ezekielian characteristic to execute several allied images along with the principal one with a view to highlighting the central contour :

> Barbaric city sick with slums,
> Deprived of seasons, blessed with rains,
> Its hawkers, beggars, iron-lunged,
> Processions led by frantic drums,
> A million purgatorial lanes,
> And child-like masses, many-tongued,
> Whose wages are in words and crumbs.

(*CP*, p. 119)

The picture of the city is vividly recalled with the other tied images — slums, hawkers, beggars, drums and purgatorial lanes — which are its essential components. The unusual character of the place is imprintingly drawn with the help of telling modifiers like barbaric, deprived, frantic and purgatorial. The line — "A million purgatorial lanes" — despite its religious undertone is evocative of a humanity immersed in poverty and gloom and undergoing with child-like faith its term of penance. Ezekiel's vision, however, is limited to the material and mundane concerns of his fellow inhabitants while Eliot harps on spiritual values. Ezekiel's disillusionment is born out of the failure to achieve worldly success while Eliot's thrust is on spiritual bankruptcy in the midst of pleasure excesses. However, the protagonist's emotional urgency is above board :

> The more he stared the less he saw
> Among the individual trees.
> The middle of his journey nears.
> Is he among the men of straw
> Who think they go which way they please?
>
> (*CP*, p. 119)

Paradox is Ezekiel's favourite trope which he invariably employs to measure the gulf between the ideal and the achieved. Used to look at things in isolation and fragments the persona searches for the serenity in 'individual trees' and not in the totality of the objects of nature as one entire and whole. The self-questioning acquires a sharper edge with the poet reaching the half way mark of his life. The comparison with Eliot's 'The Man of Straw' is not without significance in view of the persona's insubstantial assets.

Had the protagonist been born with a dull conscience the situation would have been less depressing for him. The overwhelming awareness of fallibility, of being an 'unfinished man' impels him to indulge in dreams and illusions which represent an entirely different plane of reality, the one so ardently craved and coveted by him. The anguish of unrealised ideals, the torment of having a 'fragmented view' of macrocosm trouble him continually and Ezekiel wonderfully employs metonymy which compares the persona's will to the transience of 'the morning dew' which evaporates with the rising sun. It would not be entirely out of context to point out that the Modernist poets exposed to cross-cultural interactions unfailingly realize the inadequacy of their visions. A.K. Ramanujan also expresses similar sentiments in his poem "Connect!" :

Connect,
connect, beasts with monks, slave economies
and the golden bough.

But my watchers are silent as if
they knew my truth is in fragments.[2]

The concluding stanza reverts to the much sought after scene of natural serenity though not without mythological allusions :

The garden on the hill is cool
Its hedges cut to look like birds
Or mythic beasts are still asleep.
His past is like a muddy pool
From which he cannot hope for words.
The city wakes, where fame is cheap,
And he belongs, an active fool.

(*CP*, p. 120)

The issue of the relationship between the individual and racial or the collective unconscious reverberates throughout the stanza. The allusions to garden and city instinctively recall the Garden of Eden and the City of God. The contrast between the city of Vision and the city of history "Where fame is cheap" is revealing and startling. The line "mythic beasts are still asleep" recalls Yeats's apocalyptic vision in "The Second Coming" :

but now I know
That twenty centuries of stony sleep
Were vexed to nightmare by a rocking cradle,
And what rough beast, its hour come round at last,
Slouches towards Bethlehem to be born?

The noted Indian poet and critic Adil Jussawalla's comment about "A Morning Walk" as expressing "not only his (poet's) own personal defeat but that of a whole generation"[3] is intensely thought provoking. Dwelling on the dehumanising aspect of the urban scenario it is to the credit of Ezekiel that he willingly accepts what Jussawalla terms as 'personal defeat' without being cowed down by the hellish phenomena he wades through to reach a slightly tolerable destination.

The overwhelming sense of imperfection goads the poet to undertake many a journey and quest for the enrichment of self. The theme of search for identity is developed through the extended metaphor of exploration in the poem "Enterprise" which externalises a personal problem and lends it universal validity. Through an ironically titled piece it represents the failure of an undertaking and its futility. The appropriate mood is set by the laconic detatchment of the opening stanza beginning with "It started as a pilgrimage." The quest for self began on a note of unusual delight and excitement and its comparison with pilgrimage, a traditional metaphor for the movement towards spiritual meaning, focuses on the uncommon nature of the project. However, the initial enthusiasm couldn't match the severity of the programme and the quester resorted to putting down "copious notes" under the false illusion that they might come to his rescue. To his utter dismay the teachings of various religious faiths quite often contradicted one another while he was on the lookout for harmony and amity. Such a distracting imperative begets doubt leaving the quester battered and confused. The harrowing spectacle of the pilgrim and his fellows "twice attacked," obviously gripped by doubt and fear, recalls the journey of doubting Thomases to Emmaus. The penultimate stanza vividly portrays this conglomeration of baffled and nonplussed creatures :

> We noticed nothing as we went,
> A straggling crowd of little hope,
> Ignoring what the thunder meant,
> Deprived of common needs, like soap.
> Some were broken, some merely bent.
>
> (*CP*, p. 118)

The journey that commenced with 'exalting minds' ultimately terminated with travellers drained of all hope, leaving some of them morose and grief stricken, and others completely exhausted. Their insensitivity to the message of thunder symbolic of spiritual rejuvenation only highlights their fallibility to the task they were engaged in. Far from being a meaningful expedition, this 'enterprise' is ultimately reduced to be merely topographical :

> When, finally, we reached the place,
> We hardly knew why we were there.

The trip had darkened every face,
Our deeds were neither great nor rare.
Home is where we have to earn our grace.

(*CP*, p. 118)

With the final realization dawning on them about the futility of the depressing exercise, the questers felt vexed and regret was writ large on their faces — "The trip had darkened every face." Even in the midst of a dismal plight they do underline their normal humanity which unsuccessfully strove for exceptional credence. The aphoristic last line conveys the vital truth that despite its distressing attributes home or the city of Bombay is the real destination, a place of refuge where all journeys terminate and have their meaning. It is a question of personal conformity and adjustment to one's surroundings which can be acquired and never inherited as such (cf the earlier variant 'gather' for 'earn our').

In "Case Study" the schizoid individuality of the persona is engaged in a dialogue with itself. The one voice apparently the suffering half of his fractured personality is being advised by the patient other half. One can also treat the poem as Ezekiel's dialogue of the self and the soul, a sort of deliberation between the higher and the lower selves in face of imminent catastrophe. It is a diagnostic poem loaded with moral tone, scrutinizing the life history of the persona threadbare. The opening line — "Whatever he had done was not quite right" — underscores the flawed and unfortunate course of events that were his doing. While subjecting him to an intensive investigation the poet enumerates the major items of his track record — "a foolish love-affair," "useless knowledge" gathered from "common school and rotten college," a short stint in politics, damnation in the "domestic game" called marriage and to top it all frequent vocational changes — which speak of his incoherence, inconsistency. In this lack of concentration or singleness of purpose, the protagonist reminds one of Matthew Arnold's Victorian contemporaries who were equally deficient in Scholar Gipsy's best defining human trait — 'one aim, one business, one desire'. The higher self under the mask of the narrator warns the protagonist against his rigorously conformative and painfully debilitating temperament :

He came to me and this is what I said :
'The pattern will remain, unless you break
It with a sudden jerk; but use your head...
Not all returned as heroes who had fled
In wanting both to have and eat the cake.
Not all who fail are counted with the fake.

(*CP*, p. 125)

The narrator impresses upon the protagonist the necessity of unusual courage and determination to break and challenge the stultifying routine. This will overtly involve a little bit of personal discomforts and inconveniences. Unlike Kierkegaard's hero who sinks in despair and sickness-unto-death and casts himself in the limbo of "Either/ Or," Ezekiel admonishes his hero to make a choice once forever least tempted by doubt and apprehension. Should the protagonist decide for a facelift, he must take a 'leap' from the absurd circle of ritualistic existence. The last line encapsulates the hoary wisdom that it is the gravity of the ideal howsoever unsuccessfully combated that matters and by no means the petty and paltry attainment though very much realized and accomplished.

The poem "Commitment" also embodies the theme of action and dedication as an existential imperative. The quality of fortitude and conviction assumes the form of a religious passion :

When, with sudden smile, the visions come
Inviting us to sweet disaster,
We envy saints their martyrdom
And press the accelerator.

(*CP*, p. 121)

Oxymoron is one of Ezekiel's choicest figures of speech and the 'sweet disaster' he refers to, vigorously transmits his viewpoint. Disaster can be sweet and welcome only to a man of firm resolve, undeterred by the bending quantum of insurmountable obstacles. Saints achieve their spiritual stature through a suffering of infinite proportions without ever betraying any sign of panic in the face of existential hazards. The use of the Existential term 'leap' in the second stanza — "At once we know that we must leap,/Although we have not looked ahead" — reiterates the poet's conviction that looking ahead, calculating pros and cons, invariably spoils the tenacious spirit, spelling doom for the quester.

Ezekiel's weakness for employing maxims and proverbs enables him communicate a bitter truth with light hearted gaiety. The following excerpt is an instance in point :

> Our bridges burnt, we understand
> Slow and steady wins the race,
> Or all about the bird in hand;
> But still, before the searching face,
>
> (*CP*, p. 121)

The closing stanza further elaborates on the thematic content that those who accept security in preference to threat, or are on the lookout for evading challenging situations are not necessarily always the happy ones on the earth.

Ezekiel's early enthusiasm for flesh and physical pleasures finds its reappearance in a couple of poems of *The Unfinished Man* nothing short of an adolescent hangover. His "Love Sonnet" looks back to the flora and fauna of "the hill" of "A Morning Walk" and "Urban". The ecstatic element in love forms the core of the piece, and the lovers while sharing each other's emotional excitement reflect upon the Nature outside :

> The wind has ruffled up your hair :
> We look in consort at the distant sea,
> And feel it turbulent and saltry there,
> A passionate and perpetual mystery.
>
> (*CP*, p. 120)

The poem "Event" centres round a love affair where the beloved carries a stereotyped image of the romantic and intellectual lover. In its typical didactic tone Ezekiel harps on time's sabotaging effect on love. The following stanza conveys home the truth that love degenerates into possessive sensuality and flippant indulgence with the passage of time :

> Time offers this ironic gift
> As in the middle of the way,
> They feel its flow become a drift
> And lose the will to act or pray.
>
> (*CP*, p. 122)

The poem resembles the beloved of an early piece "An Affair" (*CP*, p. 11) in her fondness for going to movies and also in her attempts to imitate art in life :

> She stroked my hair and talked away
> About a film she had admired
> A speech she heard the other day,
> And art of which she never tired.
>
> (*CP*, p. 123)

Unlike the heroine of John Keats's "La Belle Dame Sans Merci" whose echoes are too reverberating the woman in an urban society discharges the hackneyed roles : she, like her male counterpart, exists purely as an instrument and does not have personal identity. The revulsion against the girl's love arises from the protagonist's inability to be himself in her presence, to reveal himself in his strength and weakness — "I knew that both were undefined". The loss of identity and slippage of individuality are the disquietening aspects of the amorous business born of illusive ideal of oneness in Cupid's territory.

The poem "Marriage" traces the couple's diagramatic journey from the world of innocence to that of experience. Like other Ezekiel poems it delves deep into the traditional view of marriage and raises serious issues of sin and guilt. It opens with the usual emotional outburst of lovers that through love they can transcend mortality. Indian society's platitudes concerning marriage are really interesting and the married fellow is considered fortunate and privileged as a creature. The "joy of flesh and blood" momentarily appears to be all-engulfing and subsuming to the voluptuous couple. The poet recalls his own experience of undergoing the dream world of pre-lapsarian innocence :

> I went through this, believing all,
> Our love denied the Primal Fall.
> Wordless, we walked among the trees,
> And felt immortal as the breeze.
>
> (*CP*, p. 124)

This feeling of immortality under love prompted the protagonist to repeat the exercise only to invite the resultant troubles :

However many times we came
Apart, we came together. The same
Thing over and over again.
Then suddenly the mark of Cain
Began to show on her and me.

(*CP*, p. 124)

The different tone suggests the quality of the unfortunate experience and the pun on the word 'came apart' meaning sexual intercourse as well as personal separation underscores the nature of the intermittent conflict and the closeness in married life. The collapse of a relationship that depended too heavily on sexual emotion was a foregone conclusion. The allusion to the biblical figure of the guilty Cain doomed to wander on earth for the sin of killing his brother Abel conveys the idea of guilt in the spouses' psyche for their being mere sexual creatures. Both the dream and the metre are shattered and the variations in Iambic tetrametre effectively convey the image of the restrictive nature of marriage.

Ezekiel craves for an absolute relationship with the elements of nature as they symbolize the central point of man's material as well as spiritual existence in the poem "Morning Prayer." He believes that life as enigma and passion can be poetically recreated for the use of humanity. The proximity with nature will enable him perceive the objective truths of the phenomena unvitiated by narrowness, prejudice or sheer moral or intellectual strength :

In kinship with the sky
Air, earth, fire, sea—
And the fresh inward eye.

Whatever the enigma,
The passion of the blood,
Grant me the metaphor
To make it human good.

(*CP*, p. 122)

This ambition to brace himself up with the real life situations to achieve perfection of vision and art leads the poet to examine the distinctiveness of the famous artist Jamini Roy's paintings. He infers that the secret of Roy's art lies in its flow from a mind in harmony with the external world and is characterized by assent rather than hostility. The following excerpt refers to the rigorous discipline to which the great artist subjected himself to produce a piece of self-sustaining and eternal character. Once he identified his tools to portray the primitive simplicity of folk art it was an exercise of unending propositions :

> He started with a different style
> He travelled, so he found his roots.
> His rage became a quiet smile
> Prolific in its proper fruits.
>
> ("Jamini Roy," *CP*, p. 126)

The invaluable instruction drawn from Jamini Roy — "he found his roots" — further strengthened Ezekiel's conviction to stick to his locale and surroundings with a renewed vigour in the poems written hereafter.

Commenting on the poetic traits of *The Unfinished Man* which marks a definite departure from Ezekiel's first three verse-volumes, Bruce King perceptively notes the poet's successful struggle to shake off the romantic overtures :

> *The Unfinished Man* is remarkable in its self-scrutinizing psychology and polished craft. The volume moves from generalization towards the personal, from complaint to decision and ideal... Ezekiel showed how to avoid the excesses of romanticism when writing about the self and its concerns, when making art based on autobiography.[4]

Ezekiel's poetic evolution from *The Unfinished Man* onwards marks a distinct milestone of his Realist phase with the publication of *The Exact Name* (1960). In the earlier volume, the poet had been busy in self-questioning to resolve his dilemma by a more perceptive understanding of his problems. Now that he had 'found his roots' he wishes to look for 'the exact name' *i.e.*, 'the right idiom' to avoid all chances of misrepresenting reality. The poems included in this volume were written during 1960-64. They demonstrate his absorption in the indigenous scenario marked by a keen and penetrating observation with no tinge of any inhibitions. He freely looks at the Indian cultural ethos in all its multiplicity and diversity. The poem "In India" offers a kaleidoscopic picture of the native scene in four parts. One feels that the word 'India' as title, would have equally sufficed but by adding the preposition 'in,' the poet probably intended to convey as to what it means to live in India, an inescapable plunge into the remnants of colonial oppression and also in the emancipating dreams of a newly independent country with strange conglomeration of religious sects. The opening section concentrates on the wide communality nothing short of the biblical Noah's Arc :

> Always, in the sun's eye,
> Here among the beggars,
> Hawkers, pavement sleepers,
> Hutment dwellers, slums,
> Dead souls of men and gods,
> Burnt out mothers, Frightened
> Virgins, wasted child
> And tortured animal,...
>
> (*CP*, p. 131)

The use of epithets burnt out, frightened, wasted, tortured is a thought provoking commentary on the social evils that typify modern India. The poet's sense of empathy for these people gets articulated in these lines — "All in noisy silence/Suffering the place and time," attributing it to their human existence. One easily remembers these denizens of the barbaric city (*CP*, p. 119) crowding 'million purgatorial lanes' as if paying back their share of Adam's curse.

The second section is devoted to Ezekiel's childhood experiences of living and studying together with mates of different religious faiths reflected in their peculiar eccentricities and prejudices. What Ezekiel simply ignored as a boy, he ponders over in retrospect with a detached outlook. With an inbuilt moral preoccupation the poet remembers how the Roman Catholics, Anglo-Indians and Islamic boys shared with one another loose morals, unabashed boasting and hypocrisy. Their punctuality in joining services and prayers lacked genuine conviction :

> They copied, bullied, stole in pairs
> They bragged about their love affairs

They carved the table broke the chairs
But never missed their prayers.

(*CP*, p. 132)

Earnestness in prayers is meaningless if one fails to attain a certain moral level at which one refrains from committing adultery and theft. No doubt, Christianity and Islam accept the concept of prayers and there is an implicit defence on their behalf that the monotheistic concepts might be responsible for their taking an easy view of misdeeds. Through the gossipy liveliness of his pictures Ezekiel shows that religious fanaticism and diversity sink at places of common human weaknesses :

The Anglo-Indian gentleman
Drank whisky in some Jewish den
With Muslims slowly creeping in
Before or after prayers.

(*CP*, p. 132)

Surprisingly enough, the poet excludes the majority Hindu community from this account of lewdness and dishonesty, and this suppression finds its pronounced appearance in poems like "Background, Casually" when he allowed himself a still deeper and intrusive involvement in the Indian situation.

The third section offers a graphic description of Indian couples and their conduct at cultural mixing of various hues and dyes. It refers to a New Year Eve festivity joined by twentythree participants representing six different nations. This confluence of East and West is slightly inconvenient to Indian women unexposed to the Western customs, while their male counterparts conduct themselves in a becoming fashion :

The wives of Indian sit apart.
They do not drink,
They do not talk,
Of course, they do not kiss.

(*CP*, p, 133)

That Ezekiel is quick to mark the changes in social systems astutely is testified to by what he wrote in 1983 in respect of this poem :

The situation has changed, some would say for the worse, since that poem was written in 1962. The wives

> of India no longer sit apart, they drink, they talk too much and, of course, they kiss.[5]

Indianism is obvious in the phrases 'Wives of India' and 'Wooden wives' where the word women would have been a happier choice.

The fourth and final section makes a dig at British sophistry and refinement. One can sense Ezekiel's anti-colonial attitude to the British who try to endear themselves through superficial things like courtesy despite rendering graver harms like violating chastity :

> The struggle had been hard
> And not altogether successful.
> Certainly the blouse
> Would not be used again.
> But with true British courtesy
> He lent her a safety pin
> Before she took the elevator down.

(*CP*, p. 134)

Under the pretext of enjoying Western music, discussing art and literature, and above all talking of 'all the changes India needs,' the English boss finally indulges in sex to her much amazement. The effective use of understatement, surprise and irony in the last lines implies that one wanting in politeness and civility may not deserve the membership of the elite section of the world but one who is lecherous is positively unworthy of inclusion in human community.

Ezekiel's best known poem "Night of the Scorpion" was written in mid-January 1964 when the poet was staying at the University of Leeds, England, as guest speaker. He has extensively elaborated on the contingent situation behind the poem's creation. Invited to participate in a poetry recitation session, Ezekiel composed this piece on a moving childhood incident embedded in his psyche. This poetry of situation was born out of poet's mother being stung by a scorpion at night in the 1930s. Built on contrasts, the poem centres round all that followed in the wake of this tragedy. Here Ezekiel envisions ordinary reality of Indian life unmediated by cold intellect.

Having parted 'with his poison' the scorpion left the unfortunate woman to the resourcefulness of her kith and kin. The entire episode is rooted in an ingenuous simplicity of belief and spontaneous human goodwill emanating even from enemies in times of unprecedented crisis which best characterize primitive societies. The Bombay of Ezekiel's childhood was a group of several islands inhabited by local people with strange superstitions and folk beliefs. With the sophistication of civilisation, what George Orwell terms 'refinement beyond the point of civilisation', these customs might appear obsolete and uncouth. The poem has an ironic structure where the force of superstition and age-old belief is pitted against the scientific temperament. The problem of evil and its proliferating effects are deeply imprinted in the Indian psyche and even in a simple incident of scorpion bite they instinctively look for too much — sin, redemption, rebirth. The epic imagery in the following excerpt forcefully conveys the collective efforts of villagers to combat evil :

> The peasants came like swarms of flies
> and buzzed the Name of God a hundred times
> to paralyse the Evil one.
>
> (*CP*, p. 130)

Armed with candles and lanterns they search for the missing scorpion trying upon everything — their faith in God and also their secular experience to startle it by clicking of tongues. Their endeavour has its foundations in the popular belief that with the every movement of the scorpion his poison moves into the victim's blood and hence the sooner it is killed, the better. Ultimately they realise that all they could do to diminish the sins of her previous birth was simply to pray to Divine Powers. In his own subtle way the poet ponders over the common weaknesses the flesh is heir to :

> May the poison purify your flesh
> of desire, and your spirit of ambition,
> They said, and they sat around
> On the floor with my mother in the centre,
> the peace of understanding on each face.
>
> (*CP*, p. 130)

The palpably moving aspect of this phenomena is the spontaneous and incessant increase in the number of her well wishers, all restive and agitated to contribute their bit while "My mother twisted through and through/groaning on a mat." The method of trial and error continues and the protagonist's rationalist father applies his scientific knowledge by pouring paraffin on the stung toe and putting a match to it. While this huge primitive-*cum*-modern relief operation was in progress, an amazed child-observer in the poet continued helplessly looking to her mother subjected to inhuman torture. The pains subsided only after consuming its usual time defying human efforts at containing it. The poem concludes with the celebration of maternal love rooted in the Indian psyche :

> My mother only said :
> Thank God the scorpion picked on me
> and spared my children.
>
> (*CP*, p. 131)

Mother's remark signifies that it has indeed been a veritable ordeal for her and she is obviously trying to console herself that the scorpion's choice fell on her and her dear children narrowly escaped the worm's wrath.

This poem has evoked unusual adulatory response and even an otherwise unfriendly critic M.K. Naik makes the following observation which is too comprehensive to be ignored :

> While its thematic richness and its technical finesse make "Night of the Scorpion" one of the finest of modern Indian English poems, another significant aspect of it deserves special mention. It is a poem which only an Indian English poet (even though he is largely alienated from the Indian ethos, for his alienation itself is a source of poetry), could have written, since the experience and the responses to it recreated here are rooted in the modern Indian situation.[6]

Ezekiel's search for truth leads him to evolve parametres — empirical or otherwise — to reach at its core. Extremely confounding and illogical as the human reality is, the artist sometimes endeavours to define it in metaphysical terms. In "Philosophy" Ezekiel admits candidly his weakness for indulging in abstract ideas :

> There is a place to which I often go,
> Not by planning to, but by a flow

Away from all existence, to a cold
Lucidity, whose will is uncontrolled.
Here, the mills of God are never slow.

(*CP*, p. 129)

This love for cold lucidity brings him face to face with the entire non-human space-time continuum at ideational plane. The second stanza presents a graphic reflection on the flow of time. The poet considers the cataclysmic changes on the earth — natural catastrophes, wars and their ravages etc. — as painful blinks in the "sad eye of Time" which has been a helpless witness to the tragic events in man's history. This toying with philosophical-metaphysical awareness better prepares him to realise that "residues of meaning still remain" or what Hamlet tells his friend "There are more things in heaven and earth than are dreamt of in your philosophy, Horatio." The darkest myths revelling for "a final formula of light" prompt the poet to reject that variety or clarity of sight which in its intellectual burden destroys the reality of experience. One can profitably recall John Keats voicing similar sentiments "The axioms of philosophy are not true unless they are tested on our pulse." The skeletal truth reached at by philosophical ponderings is wished away by the poet who feels "What cannot be explained, do not explain." Human reality has its own parametres which alone can explore the music of life lived on empirical plane :

The mundane language of the senses sings
Its own interpretations. Common things
Become, by virtue of their commonness,
An argument against the nakedness
That dies of cold to find the truth it brings.

(*CP*, p. 129)

The coordinates of the pragmatic word improvise their commonplace interpretations of sensory occurrences. The philosophical explications, the poem forcefully argues, are inherently deficient to cope with the complexity of mundane experiences.

The poem "Perspective" explores other angles to respond to the utterly confounding reality. It can be mentioned that reality for Ezekiel is not simply surface configurations which more often than not are elusive and deceptive. In his Kohli interview, the poet has identified this piece as specifically written for personal therapy. It improvises a poetic perception with a commitment to decode and comprehend perennially upsetting dilemma. It begins with questioning the authority of saints and mystics to define human predicament on the basis of their solitary experiences of caves and groves. The intellectual approach pitiably lacks the essential prerequisite of involvement and hence inherently flawed and deficient. The urge to achieve completeness, the disquietening awareness of leading a fragmentary existence has its intangible roots :

> And yet, the body's movement in the dance
> Is what the walker dreams of, on the hill
> At dawn or nightfall, with an inward glance,
> And hears a voice insisting : find, fulfil.

(*CP*, p. 134)

The imperatives — 'find', 'fulfil' — enjoin upon the protagonist to discharge his assignment undeterred by the challenging plight. The search for the primordial sources of happiness is an onerous enterprise like the medieval Grail legend and its attendant hardships :

> Diverted from the safer paths of men,
> He rides into a marsh to see the Grail,
> Or hopes to earn a living with his pen
> Who reads the language of the world like Braille.

(*CP*, p. 134)

This poetic plunge into existence constitutes, paradoxically, a movement away from all existence. The protagonist is fully aware of his incompatibility to grapple with the task, and obviously unsure of its outcome — "the prospect of a blessing or a curse."

"Poet, Lover, Birdwatcher" is one of Ezekiel's best known anthology pieces which dwells on the delicacy of the poetic art and compares it with two other major human activities, love and birdwatching. The poet seems to have drawn on Shakespeare's famous line — "The lunatic, lover and the poet/Are of imagination all compact" — for the title with a minor substitution of birdwatcher in the place of lunatic. All these three pursuits are prompted by a uniformity of approach in that they try to decode reality as per their perception and commitment. All these enterprises are entirely different from the common run of human experience in respect of the exceptional concentration enjoined upon by them. Moving in a 'single willed direction' these questers exercise maximum caution lest their ideals deceive them. In the opening stanza Ezekiel identifies 'patience' as the secret of success that awaits these hunters of diverse dyes. A hurried and impatient quester might spoil the spirit of this rewarding venture. The poet's concept of art is reflected in the line "The best poets wait for words". The following excerpt competently links up these three enterprises where the literal and the symbolic merge :

> The hunt is not an exercise of will
> But patient love relaxing on a hill
> To note the movement of a timid wing;
> Until the one who knows that she is loved
> No longer waits but risks surrendering —
> In this the poet finds his moral proved,
> Who never spoke before his spirit moved.

(*CP*, p. 135)

The above extract pleads that an ornithologist subjects himself to a studied silence to watch a rare bird, and likewise a lover has to undergo a patient ordeal for the beloved till she "No longer waits but risks surrendering" and a patient intercourse between word and silence produces poetry. The bird-beloved-poem syndrome is tenaciously maintained in the second stanza also, which refers to other hazards associated with these unusual hobbies. For sighting an exceptional bird one has to traverse distant corners and obscure places just as love can be discovered only in remote areas like the "heart's dark floor." Women represent the fertile creative impulse and the poet calls them "myth of light/With darkness at the core." Wandering on a jig-jag track and impelled by restless inner turmoil, the poet manages to recreate his invaluable experiences of universal viability useful even for the uninitiated and incapacitated like the deaf and the blind. In short the sense or truth so found liberates the seeker but ironically enough destroys the familiar self in the process.

The concern with reality brings Ezekiel face to face with the ordinariness of most events easily ignored and unresponded to.

Ezekiel had developed great friendship with Linda Hess, an American academician of German Jewish descent in early sixties and the piece 'A Warning', is written for her. The poet warns her not to sit alone on a waterfront lest someone might push off into the Arabian Sea. Ezekiel wrote the piece 'Poem of the Separation' (*CP*, p. 194) after his break up with Linda Hess in early seventies. In "Virginal" he shows his sympathy for a spinster who has denied herself the play of her natural instincts. This poem is supposedly written for Eunice de Souza in response to her piece 'Poem for a Poet' which indirectly refers to the poet in unpleasant terms. Breathing "the bitter air of loneliness" the ageing virgin is "remote from the prospect of the wedding kiss." Even under this pathetic situation, she pretends to be happy with having her own ways in her apartment uninterfered, and obviously undisturbed. Empathising with the unfortunate lady the poet reads her suffering though the face tries to conceal it. The remnants of Lawrence's influence manifest in the concluding lines when the poet blames the lady for her undoing :

> Its gentle sadness as it slowly grew
> And crushed your liveliness, oppressed me too.
> The universe is much too small to hold
> Your longing for a lover and a child.
>
> (*CP*, p. 139)

Unlike her, the ageing male protagonist in the "Progress" tries to improve upon his early mistakes. This is a specimen of poetry of statement written in taut rhythm but highly charged. To grow wise is to fall off from 'high minded' ideals and to realise the reality and constraints of existence. While the woman of the earlier poem refused to identify her suffering, the newly acquired sagacity in this male persona mocks his former self and experience has taught him that sex is a basic human instinct and needs be satisfied unmindful of what comes one's way :

> Now he wears a thicker
> skin, upgraded from
> the goddesses of virtue
> to mocking, sexual eyes
> Whose hunger makes him wise.
>
> (*CP*, p. 141)

Ezekiel's search for the right idiom to cope with the strange reality enabled him unravel its intertwined threads in *The Exact Name*. It prompted him to identify major thrust areas for an intensive observation. More than half-a-dozen poems are devoted to an analysis of poetic process, the nature of poetic experience and the constraints on the artist to hold fast to his vocation. A pronounced feature discernible in poems like "Night of the Scorpion" and "In India" is Ezekiel's initiation into Indian cultural ethos characterised by religious multiplicity. Quite a few pieces passionately explore the attributes of physical love with a slightly changed perspective to the fair sex which is portrayed as a mixture of myth and dream. The poetic parametres so ingeniously evolved in *The Exact Name* straightforwardly equipped Ezekiel to dive deeper into his situation and surroundings.

The year 1965 is very significant in Ezekiel's poetic development in that it witnessed the publication of his two seminal writings, one critical and the other creative, besides *The Exact Name*. Ezekiel happened to go through V.S. Naipaul's much talked about and controversial work *An Area of Darkness* and wrote a review-essay under the title "Naipaul's Indian and Mine" for *The Imprint*. Later the same year, his exhaustively-discussed poem "Background, Casually," which is invariably treated as an encapsulated autobiography, was published by *Verse and Voice* (London : The Poetry Book Society). These two pieces are central to any serious discourse on Ezekiel's poetic achievements. In a way they supplement each other, and it will riot be a travesty of truth to regard "Background, Casually" as a poetic transaction of the Naipaul-essay which broadened the poet's canvas by exposing him to the crude realities of his native country debunked by the Caribbean novelist as 'an area of darkness'. It was obviously left for Ezekiel to scale the depth of this darkness or otherwise in creative terms and his realistic approach acquires a new poignancy, and sharpness hereafter.

An Area of Darkness provided Ezekiel an opportunity to dilate on his situation *vis-a-vis* Naipaul's including the complexities and amplitudes of such a predicament. He begins with questioning the very foundations of the Caribbean writer's premise :

> My quarrel is that Mr. Naipaul is often so uninvolved and unconcerned. He writes exclusively from the point of view of his own dilemma, his temperamental alienation from his mixed background, his choice, and his escape.[7]

The 'mixed background' of Trinidad born writer of the Indian origin impels Ezekiel to look at his own grounding and racial history :

> I am not a Hindu and my background makes me a natural outsider; circumstances and decisions relate me to India. In other country, I am a foreigner. In India I am an Indian.
>
> (*SP*, p. 99)

This insider-outsider matrix leads him to underline the significance of the milieu in the creative process :

> India is simply my environment. A man can do something for and in his environment by being fully what he is by not withdrawing from it. I have not withdrawn from India... Not being Hindu I cannot identify myself with India's past as a comprehensive heritage and reject it as if it were mine to reject. I can identify myself only with modern India, a place with more things in it than are dreamt of in Mr. Naipaul's philosophy.... History is behind me. I live on the frontiers of the future that is slowly receding before me, contempt for *background* impresses me as little as pride in *background*. (italics mine)
>
> (*SP*, p. 100)

It is against this backdrop of Ezekiel's concern for the root and heritage that a discussion of "Background, Casually" should appropriately be taken up. Though written and published in 1965 this piece remained uncollected until the publication of Ezekiel's next volume *Hymns in Darkness* (1976). In between *The Exact Name* and *Hymns* the poet has inserted a group of Poems (1965-1974) in the *Collected Poems* and it is perfectly justified that "Background, Casually" is analysed along with these poems, notwithstanding the fact that it was brought out in a poetic volume after a decade.

"Background, Casually" is pivotal to Ezekiel's poetic *oeuvre* because many controversies associated with his poetry stem from this piece. Something of a portrait of the artist as a young man, this piece was written for a Commonwealth Arts Festival as an explanation of his return to India, a statement of something 'often thought of but never so well expressed'. Apparently dismissive, as suggested by the modifier 'casually,' the title is a misnomer because of its consequential content which the author would have us disbelieve. The poet seems to imply that it is an account of a meaningless past, one which emanates no sense of value to the narrator, and as such he can afford to be casual about it. Comprising three sections, the poem has a circular structure — it starts with a Roman Catholic school of Bombay and terminates on the very island which is Ezekiel's 'backward place' after a four years' sojourn at London — and moves rather jerkily from one experience to another connected only by the bitterness their memory evokes. The opening line — "A poet-rascal-clown was born," — is not an entirely unintended comment on the modern poet who resembles the hero of a picaresque novel. He walks through a variety of episodes in life and it is his self that gives them some semblance of unity. His commitment to art is, therefore, sporadic, his attitude adventurous and his writings 'holiday poetry.' Recalling his childhood experiences and emotions as it were 'in tranquility,' Ezekiel begins with the long standing animosity between the Gentiles and the Jews and the disquietening aspect of the characteristic communal frenzy :

I went to Roman Catholic school,
A mugging Jew among the wolves.
They told me I had killed the Christ,
That year I won the scripture prize.
A Muslim sportsman boxed my ears.

(*CP*, p. 179)

For want of a Judaic institution this 'mugging Jew' was admitted to Antonio D'souza High School and subjected to all sorts of physical, and emotional humiliations. Hurled into a den of wolves to be perpetually interrogated and singled out as a murderer of Christ might have been a convulsive experience during the very formative years. However, and ironically enough, Ezekiel bagged a trophy in a scripture contest much to the annoyance of the classmates of other religious creeds. This persecution complex kept burgeoning with the poet realising himself as a helpless victim of religious discrimination :

> I grew in terror of the strong
> But undernourished Hindu lads,
> Their prepositions always wrong,
> Repelled me by passivity.
> One noisy day I used a knife.

(*CP*, p. 179)

'Boxed' by a Muslim sportsman, hated by Christian fanatics and maturing under the constant fear of 'Hindu lads,' Ezekiel's might have been a terribly trying proposition. That the poet's perceptive eye tenaciously observes reality is attested to by the epithet 'undernourished,' a blatant comment on the physique of the Hindu youths who derived sustenance and strength only from their overwhelming majority and not from their famished profiles marked by dullness and passivity, to lord over microscopic minorities. Afraid of the strong, he is nauseated by the lethargic and chicken-hearted fellows. These early impressions of incorrect prepositions resulted later in "Very Indian Poems in Indian English," a sense of contempt for the context and also a sense of urgency for reconciliation with the context. One can look and not unjustly, for an arrogant rather than an apologetic tone in these lines belying insolence towards natives. Gripped in a strange religious fix the poet tried to identify his spiritual moorings by exposing himself more intimately to his inherited faith Judaism besides Yoga and Zen of Indian soil. At one stage he toyed with the idea of becoming a rabbi-saint and experience spiritual illumination for himself. The consciousness of living in an imperfect and unromantic India surfaces itself in the paradoxical line — "The more I searched the less I found." Torn by his personal dilemma the protagonist, planned for his historic British trip financially helped by Padmashree Ebrahim Alkazi, his personal friend and admirer. The first section ends with Ezekiel specifically cataloguing his obsessive preoccupations — Philosophy, Poverty, Poetry — in his London basement flat.

The second section narrates how the full-blooded youth in Ezekiel living alone in the freezing winters of London was intermittently taken over by biological urges. In his characteristic ironic way the poet relates his experiences with biblical inputs for mock-serious purposes. Imagining himself as the Son of Man of the Book of Ecclesiasts, the literal Ezekiel, he attributes this infatuation for lust to some Woman understandably Eve, deeply imprinted in his monotheistic psyche as responsible for the Fall. The biblical paradigm has been employed only to underline persona's weaknesses for sex while his counterpart Jesus overcame all temptations. Though planned with high hopes of enriching the personality, the trip failed to deliver the expected goods — "I knew that I had failed/In everything, a bitter thought." The implied contrast between the conventional benefits calculated in terms of the acquisition of education and culture through such a stay abroad, and the tawdriness of the outcome in the poet's particular case is upsetting indeed. The anxiety condensed in the phrase 'bitter thought' was only an external manifestation of the emotional turmoil within caused by a strong and persistent strain of alienation of multiple dimensions. With options extremely limited for him, the protagonist decided to return to India in a huff earning his passage by undertaking menial works on an English cargo-ship. This meant simply to revive the bitter memories of unhappy moments in a voluntary bid to "laugh again at home" :

> How to feel it home, was the point.
> Some reading had been done, but what
> Had I observed, except my own
> Exasperation? All Hindus are
> Like that, my father used to say,
>
> When someone talked too loudly, or
> Knocked at the door like the Devil.
> They hawked and spat. They sprawled around.
>
> (*CP*, p. 180)

In the face of spiritual differences of alarming proportions with the mainstream culture, it was humanly impossible to feel at home in the land of his birth. An inbuilt prejudice as to the roughness and unsophistication of the Hindus with the devilish corrupting influence in the unfolding process of growth had come to stay. In his Radio talk "The Heritage of India : A Personal Statement" broadcast from the Bombay A.I.R. on 12 June 1984, Ezekiel has explicated the 'home' metaphor elaborately :

> If you have a house of your own you may keep all the windows open so that the winds of the world may play freely in it. But what happens if your house has no character, no distinctive quality... What happens if your house is not really a home in the full sense of the word, intellectually and culturally, but only a stage for rehearsing a play that is never completed and may never be performed?[8]

Howsoever despairing was the situation Ezekiel prepared himself for the *fait accompli* like a native Indian, entered into wedlock and tried his hands on several jobs and opportunities apparently to 'feel at home.' Unfortunately, the bitterness of the song of innocence was infinitely multiplied and aggravated by the harrowing experiences abroad with the possibilities of still worse things in store for him. Ezekiel for the first time outlines his pedigree and racial connections towards the close of the section which shifts the focus from the quest for assimilation to an acceptance of the actualities surrounding him.

The opening stanza of the third and final section dwells on the contribution of Ezekiels to the cultural and the historical life of the Indian nation. Adopting a rather defensive posture, the poet regrets that his family of oil crushers could not add substantially to the native ethos, the only exception in social, literary, and political terms was one of his ancestors his paternal grandfather Haskelji Israel who had fought in the Boer War of 1880s on the British behalf. Even this claim of having shared a racial past has its own pangs of conscience because it was somebody else's war fought wearing British arms, and to that extent a mercenary enterprise. That the racial history cannot absolve him of a reprehensible conscience, compelled him to go in for other options by way of ensuring his active involvement in environment. Ezekiel chose to appropriate his poetic creativity to forge spontaneous links with the soil, howsoever personally unrewarding this might turn out to be. This determination "to cash in on/The inner and the outer storms" has left its own scars on Ezekiel's poetic personality. This brings one to the celebrated stanza :

> The Indian landscape sears my eyes.
> I have become a part of it
> To be observed by foreigners.
> They say that I am singular,
> Their letters overstate the case.
>
> (*CP*, p. 181)

The Indian scenario, both physical and psychic, the poet avers, is very much part of his existence. The love-hate relationship takes on a new colour in the closing stanza with the poet accepting his predicament for want of a better alternative :

> I have made my commitments now.
> This is one : to stay where I am,
> As others choose to give themselves
> In some remote and backward place.
> My backward place is where I am.
>
> (*CP*, p. 181)

The nagging sense of failure manifested in the "remote and backward place" lurks behind all overtures of commitment so vociferously proclaimed by the poet. This is a response to the other voice, the voice of the foreigner which is so much a part of the poet's persona and with whom he is continually engaged in a dialogue. The two voices — the foreign and the Indian — provide the central dialectic in Ezekiel's poetry. William Walsh has wonderfully summed up Ezekiel's position in view of the cultural givens which shaped his sensibility, a quintessence of "Background, Casually" :

> Nissim Ezekiel in the Indian scene is a permanent expatriate, but one who has freely elected to stay. Displaced by his own spiritual past, he is in place but at a distance from, the object and his specifically Indian poetry is both inward and detached, a combination making for a peculiar strength and validity.[9]

The first piece in the Poems (1965-74) titled "Transparently" highlights Ezekiel's ideal to acquire transparent sincerity to the truth of his experience. A victim of impulses and indecision, the poet's worst oppressor is his own self — "It's fantastic/What a slave/ a man can be/who has nobody/to oppress him/except himself" — and yet this oppressing self is also the source of his poetry. The poet struggles to control the Hamlet-streak in his personality (the reverberating echo of "What a piece of work is man!" in "What a slave/a man can be") which has a penchant for ruminating on all-inclusive solutions to life's varied problems. He yearns to identify his ambivalence and settle for its resolutions :

> All I want now
>   is the recognition
> of dilemma
>   and the quickest means
>   of resolving it
>   within my limits

(*CP*, p. 150)

In the poem "In the Theatre," the growing anxiety for "transparent existence" assumes a pronounced alertness :

> I act to end the acting,
> not to be known but to know,
> to be new, to become a form and find
> my relevance.

(*CP*, p. 151)

The poem "A Small Summit" poignantly simplifies the tormenting dilemma — "either to ensure it as a fact of self-created history,/or to work upon its nearest/particulars in the light of love." He proposes to go ahead capitalising on his own perplexity :

> If nothing else, I'll keep my nerve,
> refuse the company of priests,
> professors, commentators, moralists,
> be my own guest in my own
> one-man lunatic asylum,
> questioning the Furies, my patron saints,
> about their old and new obscurities.

(*CP*, p. 153)

"After Reading a Prediction" demonstrates that Ezekiel has acquired a kind of tolerance, not a blind submission to his situation and he celebrates his very survival :

This is the place
Where I was born. I
know it
well. It is home,
Which I recognise at last
as a kind of hell
to be made tolerable.

(*CP*, p. 155)

Culturally displaced artists invariably denigrate their roots and A.K. Ramanujan regards his Hindu descent as 'hell'. The following extract implies that 'hell' though it was, it was undeniably his which he was not prepared to exchange with someone's heaven :

I must seek and will find
my particular hell only in my hindu mind :

("Conventions of Despair," *Collected Poems*, p. 34)

Ezekiel's plan of action pleads for a synthesis built on a holistic sense of self and place, different with every passing movement but permanent in its changeability :

I seek on firmer ground
to improvise my later fiction,
the fallen world
a faithful friend.

(*CP*, p. 156)

At the centre of the poet's world is an active and enduring man. One is conscious of his infinite potential and also of his ravaged limits. The poem "Happening" grapples with the paradox "A man withdrawn into himself/may be a man moving forward." The protagonist feels that his giving himself to a sense of spiritual emptiness would offset all possibilities of reintegrating the divided self which is in part built upon the very isolation and precariousness that it would reject. The synthesis which Ezekiel seeks is one to which the notion of change is essential. The poem appeals for an objectification of self and would have us believe that self withdrawal is suicidal :

I close the door and sit alone
in kinship with the world.
I am near everybody

being near myself alone....
Withdrawn into myself
I am this fever and the cause of it,
the meaning without a cure for it.

(*CP*. p. 164)

The fortitude to experience identification with society at large transforms Ezekiel into a minute observer and his perceiving self is most unsparing to persons and institutions which fall short of normal humanity. His disapproval unfailingly adopts a satirical tone as in "Three Women" and "On Bellasis Road." While the earlier poem is a satire on morally loose women who offer people not only food but love also, and thus for them, offering love is as minor an affair as offering food.

They spoke the language
of food and love
naturally
as a mother-tongue;
no problem here
or (sic) accent or of intonation.

("Three Women," *CP*, p. 151)

"On Bellasis Road" centres round a red-light locality in Bombay habitually thronged by people from all walks of life for sexual gratification. Ezekiel has a marvellous sense of colour as demonstrated in the following excerpt imaging a lowly prostitute :

I see her first
as colour only,
poised against the faded
red of a post-box :
purple sari, yellow blouse,
green bangles, orange
flowers in her hair.

(*CP*, p. 188)

The protagonist suffers from a sort of timidity lurking under the shadow of false morality and fails to engage her attention. Since her customers do not carry the burden of traditional moral taboos in approaching her, they are most welcome and anxiously awaited in her den :

She doesn't glance at me,
Waiting for her
hawker or mill-worker,
coolie or bird-man
fortune-teller,
pavement man of medicine
or street-barber on the move.

(*CP*, p. 189)

Quite a few poems like "The Truth about Dhanya" and "Ganga" have been devoted to other destitute segments of society often ignored by the elitist class.

The observation of reality reveals layers within layers of social structure marked by their own peculiar values. The extension of personal self into the life around enables Ezekiel to single out people and places where hypocrisy is a rule rather than exception. The poem "Guru" exposes the so-called religious healers with proven expertise in cheating people. That Ezekiel should dwell on this unhealthy social disgrace exhibits his growing affirmation of inseparability from one's ethos and one's surroundings, howsoever fraudulent and disgusting they might be. The spiritual development of Gurus demonstrates a career uniformity in that they attain sainthood via sinfulness. In a humorous vein the poet looks for a potential Guru in every passer-by including his good self "dropping our follies/like old cloths or creeds" when the opportune moment knocks at the threshold. Even after the so-called spiritual elevation the Gurus retain their instinctive weaknesses and bring disrepute to the position which they so vociferously profess :

But then we learn
the saint is still a faithless friend,
obstinate in argument,
ungrateful for favours done,
hard with servants and the poor,
discourteous to disciples, especially men,
condescending, even rude
to visitors (except the foreigners)
and overscrupulous in checking
the accounts of the *ashram*.

(*CP*, p. 192)

A peep into the private life of such saints is unredeemably despairing and the poem closes with the telling satire :

> If saints are like this,
> What hope is there then for us?

This excerpt reminds one of Chaucer's line, "That if gold ruste, what shall iren doo?" from *The Prologue*. From the stylistic point of view, however, this overtly moralistic end spoils the beauty of the piece. This ought to have been left for the reader to ruminate over.

This attack on mushrooming God-men, specially in the metropolitan cities, with prospective victims in the credulous and gullible, brings one to mark the meaningless formality and sophistication of an elitist society in "Goodbye Party for Miss Pushpa TS" first of his 'Indian English Poems' written during his stay at Mithibai College in 1967. Executed in a dramatic monologue, this incisively satirical piece presents an authentic picture of a typical Indian life-situation. The gentle irony pervades the entire poem and reveals the poet's empathy with the speaker. Linguistic and grammatical mistakes simply accentuate the truthfulness of the situation :

> You are all knowing, friends,
> What sweetness is in Miss Pushpa.
> I don't mean only external sweetness
> but internal sweetness.
> Miss Pushpa is smiling and smiling
> even for no reason
> but simply because she is feeling.
>
> (*CP*, p. 190)

Hyperbolic sentiments are quite common on formal occasions and people even remotely acquainted with the quest of the ceremony, exhaust all superlatives without meaning them. The situation is demeaning to Miss Pushpa who, as per social propriety, is required to listen to such speeches and is expected to "do summing up" afterwards. Ezekiel makes a dig at the Indians' craze to visit abroad for career prospects and this can be viewed as a post-colonial resistance.

"How the English Lesson Ended" provides another instance of Ezekiel's post-colonial overtures in that it decries the Indian psyche to treat English as a prerequisite of social respectability, besides being a telling snap-shot of the native scenario. It takes the reader to a Muslim family where parents want their daughter to be tutored in English, her Achille's heel, at the matriculation, she failed thrice to get through. Unfortunately, this enterprise fails in its mission when the girl is discovered to be enjoying obscene pictures during the tuition hours. The morally conscious parents abruptly stop the so-called tuition and she is married off ultimately. The tutor in the protagonist fails to guess the inside story until his mother takes him to task :

> They probably decide I made advances,
> and almost hint as much
> to my poor mother, who's outraged.
> There is gratitude for you, she says,
> *That girl will never get a husband*!
>
> (*CP*, p. 201)

The simple fact that his amorous advances, genuine or alleged, were known to his mother make the persona extremely embarrassed and ashamed of. It is specifically an Indian trait, and even V.S. Naipaul prefers to be silent over his sex life lest it should expose him to his mother :

> I cannot write sex...I would be embarrassed
> at the moment of writing. My friends would laugh.
> My mother would be shocked and with reason.[10]

As part of his commitment to treat of ordinary life, Ezekiel habitually highlights underlying pathos as in "The Railway Clerk" and "Entertainment." "The Railway Clerk" is a touching picture of a monotonous life lived on barest means. The protagonist engulfed in the existential dilemma accentuated by the drudgery of the job is prone to get annoyed with people he deals with. A victim of official bossism and working in inhygienic conditions he is pricked by his failure to meet his wife's simple demands to arrange for his children's proper education and to satisfy the expectations of the kith and kin. While finding fault with his situation he images himself as a captive of an inhuman institution :

My wife is always asking for more money.
Money, money, where to get money?
My job is such, no one is giving bribe,
While other clerks are in fortunate position
and no promotion even because I am not graduate

I wish I was bird.

(*CP*, p. 184)

The Indianness of the poem is pronounced not only in the subject matter but in syntax and lexis as well. The dropping of articles before common nouns is a jocularly Indian habit and the pathos of the persona's life is considerably relieved by the slightly comical use of the language. The piece borders on sympathy rather than ridicule and the authenticity of experience gets powerfully emphasised.

While the Railway clerk is a lowly paid employee struggling for survival reluctantly, "Entertainment" derives its poignancy from the pathetic plight of the monkey-wallahs. It is a common experience to find the "Master of Ceremonies" moving around with a couple of monkeys for show and thus earn his livelihood. "Naked to the Waist" he cracks whip, drums frenzy and tries all tricks to earn applause and also copper coins. Gradually people collect together to watch the monkey-show but apathetically enough the show ends with the showman's acquisition of the smallest coins. It is worth noting that Ezekiel's sympathies are not confined simply to the human in the showmaster but also to the dumb monkeys who are in turn treated unfeelingly by him :

Only the monkeys are sad,
and suddenly
the baby begins to cry.
Anticipating time for payment,
the crowd dissolves.
Some, in shame, part
with the smallest coin they have.
The show moves on.

(*CP*, p. 194)

The rhythm of life continues through all helter and skelter, and Ezekiel's well known poem "Island" is a satirical account of the quality of life lived in the city of Bombay. Island is a traditional symbol of alienation in poetry and given Ezekiel's cultural marginality, the poet and the landscape mirror each other. The protagonist feels that the enormous expansion of the city in terms of slums and, skyrocketting buildings together precisely reflects his castaway status. It is only by finding his way in the island city that he may find his way into himself — "I am here to find my way in it." Living in the midst of people feverishly engaged in cut-throat competitions, the protagonist's perplexity bursts forth thus :

> I hear distorted echoes
> of my own ambiguous voice
> and of dragons claiming to be human.

(*CP*, p. 182)

The distorted sounds and echoes could also suggest Caliban's island but the native cannot follow his salvation :

> How delight the soul with absolute
> sense of salvation, how
> hold to a single willed direction?
> I cannot leave the island,
> I was born here and belong.

(*CP*, p. 182)

A willing captive of the place, he hurries to daily business instead of chasing the absolute his soul aspires after :

> Even now a host of miracles
> hurries me to daily business,
> minding the ways of the island
> as a good native should,
> taking calm and clamour in my stride.

(*CP*, p. 182)

This 'calm and clamour' recalls "kindred clamour close at hand" of "Urban" (*CP*, p. 117). It is remarkable that even a long gap of thirteen years that elapsed between the composition of these two poems, Ezekiel's initial attachment to the city remains intact despite its disenchanting features he uninhibitedly exposes. In fact, Ezekiel's poetry inhabits middling ground between a skyscraper and a slum; neither staggering nor hyperbolic, but equally it never fails to overwhelm the reader in its warmth, its humanity and above all its homeliness.

This presentation of reality marked by an overt disapproving tone brings one to the essential biological reality with its roots in love and sex. "Motives" dwells on the details of anatomy — skin, eyes, breasts, thighs — of the beloved as if she were a landscape or a piece of painting. In its sensuous appeal it recalls early Ezekiel poems :

> The eyes are large,
> so are the breasts—
> does size matter?
> I don't think so.
> Your thighs are full and round,
> thin and flat I'd love them too.
>
> (*CP*, p. 154)

In the piece titled "Tone Poem", the followers of "animal faith" as the lover and the beloved are, he begins his affair with a reference to breasts : "Your breasts are small, tender like your feelings." (*CP*, p. 203)

Even a "Poem of the Separation" based on Ezekiel's breakup with, Linda Hess, helps the poet recall how their love remained unaffected by the violent happenings in the external world — "When the bombs burst in Kashmir;/ my life had burst/ and merged in yours." While apparently citing parts of the beloved's letter verbatim, he reverts to his earlier infatuation with fire as a sex symbol :

> Your latest letter says :
> 'I am enclosing
> Ramanujan's translation
> of a Kannada religious poem :
> "The Lord is playing
> with streamers of fire."
> I want to play with fire.
> Let me get burnt.'
>
> (*CP*, p. 196)

To perceive beyond the tangible reality punctuated with empirical determinants is a Herculean task which Lord Shiva divinely achieves through his third eye. Ezekiel's poem "Testament" is concerned with the ways of 'seeing,' looking beyond the palpable and the obvious. It pleads that the process begins with memory leading to the "silent hour" of contemplation and the "moment of winging" in which the event is reborn. The invisible presence of imagination resurrects memory through its radiating potency. The very process is so secretive that "you may not see it happening./ You only know the norm." The transforming imagination can find a contemporary relevance in a remembered private or public event and can transmute the memory into a pattern opening the event to interpretation. The poet feels that the essential truths of life can be comprehended only by creative redemption :

Unredeemed,
we never learn the art
of bringing up-to-date
The essential truth of old performances,
abandoning the costumes, make-up,
settings, stage directions.

(*CP*, p. 159)

This tranquil process of creativity and growth forms the thematic content of the piece "Lawn." It begins with a very common weakness to confine one's observation simply to the actual, never looking beneath one's nose, which is an incomplete understanding of the macrocosm. The protagonist regrets his ignorance of the developing process of a lawn which includes a gardener's labour, a piece of land, water and seed, and over and above all these "patience at the root." Once he is inclined to dive deeper into the mystery of growth, he could realise the esemplastic power which intuits

a silence in the depths a stir of growth
an upward thrust
a transformation —
botanic turmoil
in the heart of earth.

(*CP*, p. 162)

This sprouting event is symbolic of a religious revelation which is at the heart of this poem. With the grass becoming too long and the lawn wild, the skilled gardener does periodic cutting to ensure its growth and attraction. The poem closes on a serene thought that everything in this macrocosm has to "maintain its ritual/of mortality." The poem titled "The Room" centres round the poet's place of existence and his predicament. Concentrating on this metaphor of poetic self the protagonist attributes the urge to recreate a microcosm to a nagging discontent with the existing state of affairs in actual life. The hard earned doctrines and the poet's consciousness of his stance cause him considerable distress :

> One cannot stare for long
> at nothing, or contemplate a view
> Where only obstacles reflect
> the view within. I have to name anew
> the things I see.

(*CP*, p. 206)

The creation of an individual artistic universe does infrequently derive sustenance from non-native experiences as in Ezekiel's case itself. In 'London" he immortalises the dormitory once inhabited by him :

> Sometimes I think I'm still
> in that basement room,
>
> a permanent and proud
> metaphor of struggle
>
> for and against the same
> creative, self-destructive self.

(*CP*, p. 199)

That Ezekiel was born with a strange providence to contain and amalgamate diametrically opposed propositions is also borne out by "Poster Poems." In a typical Jewish vein he pontificates on his situation :

> I've never been a refugee
> except of the spirit,
> a loved and troubled country
> Which is my home and enemy.

(*CP*, p. 209)

Tired of human fallibility and bewildering predicament, the poet is in an interrogating mood questioning the very design of his Creator in "Theological." It is a treatise on the doctrinology of religion and attempts to treat its postulates in a layman's terms. The logic of theology is too momentous to be easily grasped :

> I've stripped off a hundred veils
> and still there are more
> that cover your Creation.
> Why are you so elusive?

(*CP*, p. 156)

If the word of God is intended to illumine the reasons for existence, why then is God so elusive? The enigmatic nature of God alienates Him from humanity. The religious fervour loses its purpose and meaning when infected with corrosive doubt. Weariness from an unproductive search — "I am tired/of irony and paradox/of the bird in the hand/and the two in the bush...of the Many/and even, yes,/ of the One" — for an evasive meaning leads to nihilism. The anger of the poet explodes thus at the end :

> What a terrible situation
> Your Divine Love has created.
> Or has Something Other
>   Created it
>   and you are
>   old trying
>   to save it?

(*CP*, p. 158)

Ezekiel's "The Egoist's Prayers" has an overt echo of the *Gita* where the universal egoist in the poet comically engages himself in a dialogue with God. His situation reminds one of Arjuna's where the veteran warrior seeks Lord Krishna's advice in the moments of intense personal crisis on the battlefield. Ezekiel does not conceive of God in terms of His Olympian aloofness, or as an awesome supernatural reality. There is in him a Blakean strain of humanising God. The poet speaks to Him casually and informally like a friend and often his expression is punctuated with banter and irony. It was originally titled "Poster Prayers" and exhibited at Gallery Chemould from 10-20 March 1975. Persona is that of the self-centred self, which is strong in all of us. The tension and the dialogue between that self and the protagonist's other self provide the inspiration for the poem. Ezekiel's approach to religion has ever been unconventional, irrepressibly ironic and incessantly comic despite his avowed acceptance of Judaism in the later years. The resultant emotion here is not of passive submission but of defiant questioning.

Comprising seven pieces, it is a masterly attempt at appropriating scriptural truths in contemporary idiom. Equipped with paradoxes and inversions as stylistic tropes, the poet presents his case before his silent God. The opening prayer in mock modesty accepts suffering as the inescapable human predicament. The protagonist feels that God had better be reminded of his duty to redeem the vicious man of his sin :

From this Human Way of Life
Who can rescue Man
If not his Maker,
Do thy duty, Lord.

(*CP*, p. 212)

Adverting to the *Gita's* famous doctrine of disinterested action, the protagonist craves God's indulgence over his inability to suppress entirely his hunger for such basic pleasures of world as sex, love, success. The following passage is a cryptic comment on the impossibility of resigning oneself to pure action without craving for compensation :

No, Lord,
not the fruit of action is my motive.
But do you really mind half a bite of it?
It tastes so sweet,
and I'm so hungry.

(*CP*, p. 212)

The inherent contrast between God's and man's choices is the burden of the fourth prayer where the irreverent devotee is willing to oblige his Creator only if their wills coincide. In the fifth prayer the poet ridicules the biblical concept of transcending all material concerns :

Let me be, O Lord,
the Camel of the Higher Income Group

Who passes smoothly through
the eye of that needle.

(*CP*, p. 213)

The poet seems to be only making a case for revamping the Covenant between the Lord and man. Why won't 'the Camel of Higher Income Group' pass 'smoothly through the needle' which would let one of the poor so readily and smoothly? The rich, too, might deserve the treatment promised to the poor. Though closing on a too facile and glig note, "The Egoist's Prayers" reiterates Ezekiel's conviction to become a component of native stream :

Confiscate my passport, Lord,
I don't want to go abroad.
Let me find my song
Where I belong.

(*CP*, p. 213)

Himself a critic of no small stature, the poet rated this piece artistically deficient but "the Prayers, I feel, are in my true voice, even when not poetry of a high or even moderately high order."[11] It anticipates "Hymns in Darkness" where Ezekiel demonstrates a richer and more comprehensive account of his spiritual allegiance.

"Hymns in Darkness" is regarded by common consent, as Ezekiel's seminal poem where his spiritual aptitude is best reflected in all its diversity. It would be in the fitness of things to linger awhile on what the poet said about his religious conviction at the ripe age of sixty in his radio-talk referred to earlier, before an analysis of the piece is undertaken :

> Judaism was my religion but I not only rejected it in early youth but all religions with it. That I am today back into Judaism in a small way and accept the core of all historical religions is a different story.... Even when I was an atheist and, therefore, against all religions, I had no problems in the appreciation of their mystical tradition (p. 72).

The appreciation of Hindu mystical tradition was undertaken by Ezekiel in a passionate way in mid seventies with its fruition in this poem. Living in a room alone, the poet reminisces, he would turn out the lights and compose poetry in his head related to the Vedic Hymns he was reading in English translation.

It is not a mere coincidence that 'darkness' occurs as a principal term both in Naipaul's controversial travelogue *An Area of Darkness* and in Ezekiel's "Hymns in Darkness." By darkness the celebrated novelist means the external unhealthy manifestations like illiteracy and ignorance that characterised his ancestors' country during his visit in the early sixties. His vision was confined simply to the surface realities and could not penetrate the deeper connotation of 'darkness' which is central to the Indian spiritual experience — *Tamaso ma jyotirgamaya* (Lead me from darkness to light). In Ezekiel's poem it literally means the darkness of the fallen spirit in contrast to those who live by spiritual illumination. Negatively it may mean a mystic way or state of salvation — the Divine can be unknowable darkness as well as light. Developed into sixteen sections, the poem is a sum total of Ezekiel's religious musings, an assemblage of fragments scattered throughout his early poetry. Because of the use of persona and distance, affirmations of the self can be ironic confessions of guilt.

The opening hymn concentrates on the quality of humility which is first casualty with a self-centred person. To overcome one's ego and lead a peaceful life is an impossibility :

> Self-esteem stunts his growth. He has not learnt
> how to be nobody.
> All his truths are outside him,
> and mock his activity.

(*CP*, p. 217)

The second piece argues that to be a human being is to live in perpetual self-deception. The poet is critical of yogic practices which aim at exploiting powers for self-aggrandisement :

> He speaks with his own voice. He listens
> with the Third ear. He sees
> with the eye
> in the centre of his forehead.

(*CP*, p. 218)

One recalls the poet's instinctive allergy to such practices "I don't want the Yogi's concentration" ("A Poem of Dedication," *CP*,

p. 40) — which focus attention on the point between the eyebrows (supra-consciousness) as if to claim omniscence. The third hymn further dismisses people possessed of self-interest prone to appropriate situations to their best advantages.

The moralist in Ezekiel adopts a more didactic tone in the fourth hymn. The gap between abstract theorising and practical choice is its focal content. Whatever roles the protagonist accepted, he proved a miserable failure due to this hypocrisy. All he can do is to take it as his *fait accompli*, and attribute his fiasco to the conspiracy of circumstances. Hymns from V to X dwell on familiar human follies with which man maintains "unredeemable relationships". They convincingly argue that man basically remains flawed and corrupt — notwithstanding his age, marital status, profession and personal profile. The XI hymn affirms man's humanity and criticises the unchanging nature of his Creator :

> The absentee landlord,
> The official of all officials.
>
> The oppressor who worships God
> and the oppressed who worship God
>
> are victims of the Enemy.

(*CP*, p. 222)

The following hymn spells out the advantages of darkness which in the long run turns out to be superior light. It pleads that there are several secrets which are preserved by darkness and distorted by light :

> The darkness has its secrets
> Which light does not know.
>
> It's a kind of perfection,
> While every light
> distorts the truth.

(*CP*, p. 223)

Here the importance of light is not negated or excluded but instead darkness has been treated as a variety of light, certainly not the absolute one which would demand a surrender of a large part of one's humanity.

In the remaining four hymns, the point of view changes in that the first person singular assumes the role of a narrator and engages himself later on in a conversation with someone, who undoubtedly is the poet's own self. The XIII hymn is overtly autobiographical, a sort of balance sheet of Ezekiel's gains and losses and the quality of life lived "partly in exile from himself,/partly in a prison of his own making." It closes with the poet toying with the dichotomy between darkness and light :

I saw him cheerful
in the universal darkness,
as I stood grimly
in my little light.

(*CP*, p. 224)

The XIV and XV sections are devoted to further underlining the human constraints. The last hymn poses the fundamental problem of human mortality and the attempts at mitigating, much less changing its bite. It pleads that salvation is a question neither of belief nor of unbelief. It is given only to earnest and assiduous seekers to discover essential reality and its mysterious ramifications. Regardless of how the world was made, one can enjoy its miracles wrapped in peculiar experiences :

All you have
is the sense of reality,
Unfathomable
as it yields its secrets
slowly
one
by
one.

(*CP*, p. 225)

The impact of the Vedic hymns on Ezekiel's psyche is deeply imprinted because he argues for rejoicing the mystery of life unperturbed by ratiocinative systems of faith and faithlessness. What is valuable in the last analysis, the "Hymns" aver, is not any metaphysical system as such but the very experience of living this life. This eternal hankering after experience, insatiable eagerness to advance, is what confers value and meaning on life.

The foregoing analysis of the poems written by Ezekiel in the middle phase of his career conveniently named the "Realist" evidences significant traits of his poetic personality. It began with a proclaimed commitment to his surroundings in the very opening of the sixties and terminated with the publication of "Hymns in Darkness" in 1976. With the rejection of early Romantic enthusiasm, Ezekiel had to formulate his poetic idiom afresh to cope with the challenging external reality. Despite being city-bred and urban in sensibility, the poet tried to reach out to the centre-stage of cultural ethos in poems like "Night of the Scorpion," "Island" and "In India." Critical by temperament he has given an uninhibited expression to native concerns in his characteristic ironic tone. His diatribe against certain accepted values and institutions has earned him the annoyance and displeasure of many a critic who matter in the Third World Literature. With the onset of seventies Ezekiel was drawn towards spiritual and metaphysical concerns more pronouncedly, and in the poems like "Theological," "The Egoist's Prayers" and "Hymns in Darkness" he has derived immensely from basic Hindu scriptures. This trend was the natural sublimation of his avowed rootedness to his 'backward place.' The impact of vedic hymns gave a new dimension to his poetic sēlf which was better prepared to enjoy the bliss of earthly existence. The poems written since 1976 are marked by an unusual fervour and love for humanity which is the concern of the chapter that follows.

REFERENCES

1. McCutchion, David. "Examen de Midi," *The Miscellany*, 29 (Oct. 1968), 71.
2. A.K. Ramanujan, *The Collected Poems* (Delhi : OUP, 1995), p. 178.
3. "New Poetry" in William Walsh ed. *Readings in Commonwealth Literature* (London : Orient, 1973), p. 80.
4. *Modern Indian Poetry in English* (Delhi : OUP, 1987), p. 98.
5. "What Is Indian in Indo-English Poetry?" *Osmania Journal of English Studies*, 19 (1983), 56.
6. "The Tale is in the Sting," *Dimensions of Indian English Literature* (New Delhi : Sterling, 1984), pp. 39-40.
7. "Naipaul's India and Mine" in Ezekiel, *Selected Prose* (Delhi : OUP, 1992), p. 86.
8. *Setu*, 1, 3 (1985), 71-72.

9. "Two Indian Poets," *Literary Criterion*, 11, 3 (Winter 1974), 3-4.
10. Here quoted from Boris Ford (ed.), *New Pelican Guide to English Literature*, Vol. 8 (Harmondsworth : Penguin Books, 1983), p. 323.
11. Quoted in P.K.J. Kurup, *Contemporary Indian Poetry in English* (New Delhi : Atlantic Publishers, 1991), p. 92.

5

The Humanist Phase

As has been demonstrated in the preceding chapter, Ezekiel's study of the seminal Hindu scriptures like the *Vedas*, the *Upanishads* and the *Gita* combined with his racial faith, equipped him with a still sharper perspective to look at the human situation with an unusual involvement. While brooding on the design and mosaic of the macrocosm he could now perceive in it an exceptional charm inviting him to enjoy and celebrate life despite its transitoriness and fallibility. The poems written since the publication of *Hymns in Darkness* reflect Ezekiel's humanistic preoccupations in that they invariably accept failure and frustration as part and parcel of human existence which has many more things to revel in. With the growing age, the poet assumes the role of a grand old man impelled by an urge to bless humanity and in that one can visualise the sublimation of the early Ezekiel ambition to achieve "a human balance humanly" in preference to "the perfect charity of saints" and "the tyrant's endless power" ("A Poem of Dedication," *CP*, p. 40). The relentless pursuit of objectification and an impelling drive to come out of the self acquire a dimension as never before, a magnitude of concerns which betray the typical Indian trait of *Vasudhaika Kutumbakam* (The whole world as family). The poetic graph since the publication of *Hymns in Darkness* typically demonstrates the spiritual ambience almost overshadowing other commitments. Even the realistic social pictures have lost their usual ironic tone and cynical bite in these latest poems comprising Ezekiel's humanist phase from 1976 till date.

To begin with the mildly satirical pieces in *Latter-Day Psalms*, one finds Ezekiel recording his impressions on observable realitv in two ways : either by picking up a symbolic individual who represents an important segment of Indian society, or by exposing the weaknesses of certain institutions. The piece 'The Patriot' from "Very Indian Poems in Indian English" is a gentle satire on the Gujarati-influenced English often used in Bombay. It exploits not only the 'Indianism' in subject matter but also the Indian way of thinking in English which however badly spoken is a colonial remnant in the Indian psyche as a status symbol. It unravels the untramelled heterogeneity of Indian sub-continent as manifested in its political, social and cultural systems. The protagonist is the portrait of a confused mind which has withdrawn into a parody of Gandhism, mistaking platitudes for thought and action. Apparently showing his willingness to found a Ram Rajya on Gandhian pattern, he betrays a propensity to consume native values — "Ancient Indian Wisdom is 100% correct./I should say even 200 per cent correct." Proud of his aptitude "To improve my English Language," he assumes the leadership of the masses under the vanity of uprightness. Ezekiel's proneness to literary pilferage is pronounced in the following excerpt in its overt echoes in Brutus's celebrated speech in Shakespeare's *Julius Caesar* :

> Friends, Romans, Countrymen, I am saying
> (to myself)
> Lend me the ears.
> Everything is coming —
> Regeneration, Remuneration, Contraception.
> Be patiently, brothers and sisters.
>
> (*CP*, p. 237)

As a true Gandhian he asserts, "I'm the total teetotaller, completely total," and advises his followers to go in for a glass of *lassi* with a little salt and have a *swadeshi* sip. As a conscientious patriot he is rightly worried over boundary disputes with Pakistan and China which ultimately lead him to "think of prospects of world peace." In his characteristic humorous vein Ezekiel lets him not forget the brewing native discontent and regional differences eating into the very vitals of Indian body-politic :

> In India also
> Gujaratis, Maharashtrians, Hindiwallahs
> All brothers —

Though some are having funny habits.
Still, you tolerate me,
I tolerate you,
One day Ram Rajya is surely coming.

(*CP*, p. 238)

The irony implicit in the intransitive verb 'tolerate' hints at the mutual infighting and intermittent communal riots ultimately dying down taking their own toll of human lives. The poem closes with the protagonist offering a standing invitation to the audience for an obliging visit as per their convenience.

The second piece titled "The Professor" registers the poet's unhappiness with the members of the teaching community. It would not be entirely unjust to look for Professor Ezekiel in the protagonist Professor Sheth, despite his different discipline of Geography. As an insider fully conversant with his colleagues' allergy to retirement, he makes the protagonist express his reluctance — "I am retired, though my health is good." This plea to continue in service on the ground of good health offers a victim's perspective (though light heartedly) to service conditions. In the caricature of Professor Sheth Ezekiel intends to underline by implication certain noble attributes unconsciously imprinted on an Indian mind. A teacher or professor is looked upon as the custodian of all human virtues and ideals, a model, a sort of beacon of light for teeming millions instinctively entrapped in their existential dilemmas. As the ill-luck would have it, the protagonist prides over his children's positions who "Are well settled in life." He never tires of boasting of his worthies, one a sales manager and the other a Bank manager, "Both have cars." The sense of regret at having chosen an impoverishing academic career as opposed to the lucrative administrative positions that guarantee handsome perks and privileges can be unmistakenly marked. Narrowly confined to kith and kin, his complacency reaches a new dimension with the daughters — Sarala and Tarala — having nice boys as their husbands. Unredeemably given to glorifying his self as superannuated people are wont to, he loves to boast of his physique — "No diabetes, no blood pressure, no heart attack" — and credits it to "sound habits in youth." It is rather unfortunate that a professor should be so unconcerned about the miseries in his neighbourhood and the world outside. His pretended modesty is reflected in the following closing lines :

> If you are coming again this side by chance,
> Visit please my humble residence also.
> I am living just on opposite house's backside.
>
> (*CP*, p. 239)

If the vision of a professor whether coming from the humanities or the sciences is so myopic and straightened, he is a professor in the literal sense of the term, one who professes what one never practises. Entering the academics simply to earn one's bread is to miss its real import and the challenging obligations it enjoins upon the incumbent. The use of Indianism — 'this side,' 'my humble residence' (the literal translation of *garibkhana*), 'opposite house's backside' — adds infinitely to the humorous content of the poem.

If in "The Professor" Ezekiel satirises the profession of teaching, "Warning : Two Sonnets" is devoted to a searching criticism of a poet's vocation. The title 'Warning' is a sort of caution to the devotees of Muse who nurse false illusions about themselves. The poets are generally believed to be uncommon creatures endowed with a unique faculty to look into 'the light of things.' Ezekiel dismisses this concept of "a special gift," as "falsehood whispered to a child." The poet feels that the contours of reality are too baffling to be precisely expressed. Given the people's expectation of him he feels perturbed at his failure to justify his profession :

> The images he cannot find
> haunt his unrevealed subconsciousness.
> A plain language lets him down.
>
> (*CP*, p. 233)

Unlike Christ whose suffering brought him godhood, the poet's cross results in the cheap praise of "friendly people easily impressed/ but never wholly taken in." The extraordinary aura of being a seer and sage which the poet unconsciously carries with him turns out to be something hopelessly disappointing — "They know the sage is probably a clown." The connotation of the word 'clown' is a throwback to "Background, Casually" — "A poet-rascal-clown was born." The second sonnet advises the poet to be selective both in writing poems and in accepting praise for them. He mentions quite specifically that the readers are a cunning lot and it requires astuteness to distinguish genuine admiration from the insincere one :

> ... customers
> are shrewd, even when they don't complain
> they doubt, and sense their discontent.
>
> (*CP*, p. 233)

The people are prone to suspect a poet's credentials and more often than not he is believed to be "one of those who cheat with words/ instead of money." The fraudulence and fabrication of these people is detected only by critic corps who take them to task for distorting reality. The poem ends on an advising note to the poetic community to accept the reality :

> Come, confess, and do not talk of God.
> Your vanity is not as wretched as your style.
>
> (*CP*, p. 234)

In the opening piece "Undertrial Prisoners" from "Song for Nandu Bhende" Ezekiel disapproves of existing colonial Jail laws with their complex and circuitous procedures to deliver justice especially from the humanistic point of view. The undertrial prisoners have to rot in jails for years together before trials get initiated against them. The entire spirit of the poem centres round the idea 'hate the sin and not the sinner.' Almost empathising with the prisoner the poet pities him for not having enough money to get him bailed out. He seems to have been put behind bars for committing a cognizable offence long back. The first person singular persona 'I' becomes 'we' in the third stanza and the poet holds him responsible for law's delay because he is a part of the system :

> We have our rules
> made long ago
> he's got to wait,
> the laws say so.
> it's not our fault
> he lives in jail.
> he did something wrong
> and he can't pay bill.
>
> (*CP*, p. 241)

The poet thinks of the criminal essentially as a human being with his own share of omissions and commissions and he has no objection to his being tried under the laws of the land. He however feels for the suffering creature because poverty in his case has become a double curse as it forced him to do a wrong which could not be righted in a pecuniary situation. The poet implicitly suggests that the pre-Independence legal norms formulated by the imperialists to suit their conveniences need to be recast to administer justice both in letter and spirit. The last line — "the Law must take its time" — is a parody of the oft-saying 'the Law must take its course.' The poem lays all stress on the quick and speedy disposal of litigations to ensure the earliest relief to the victim and also the quickest punishment to the culprit with the barbarity of his heinous crime still fresh in his memory.

In the VIII piece in "Ten Poems in Greek Anthology Mode," Ezekiel exhibits a gesture of rebuffing colonial intricacies. The red tapism best characterised colonial strategies and this satire on officialdom demonstrates how persons entrapped in it fail to distinguish between their office duties and their personal lives. Theirs becomes a mechanical conduct so much so that even a solemn institution like marriage calling upon emotional impulses gets an officious treatment. Instructions of the female clerk to the prospective husband, a neighbour at the moment to apply in triplicate for marriage exhibit the complete drying up of the human element in either sex. As a humanist Ezekiel pities such a distortion of human personality :

> When the female railway clerk
> Received an offer of marriage
> From her neighbour the customs clerk,
> She told him to apply in triplicate,
> And he did.

(*CP*, p. 275)

Ezekiel attacks the vulgarity and impiety associated with the holy institution of marriage in the poem "Jewish Wedding in Bombay." Overtly recalling the rituals of his marriage with Daisy Jacob way back on 23 November 1952, the poet finds fault with many a rite which hardly conform to the spirit of the solemn occasion. Ezekiel's greatness as a poet lies in his ironic art of transforming the average and commonplace into something exceptionally compelling and thought-provoking. He remembers how his mother-in-law was shedding tears, though enjoying every moment, because it was customary to do so. As a sensible groom the poet offered consolations mistaking convention for reality only to be laughed at by the prospective bride. Written in a bantering mood, the poem exploits even the minutest tricks resorted to by the bridal host and his men to poke fun at the master of the ceremony. As a 'modern' but modest boy, the protagonist had no expectations in dowry, a fact which simply amused the bride's father over the naivete of the boy. He enumerates the details of the ceremony as per Mosaic Law wherein breaking of a common glass of grape juice for the would-be weds signifies the nuptial knot. Ezekiel feels that contrary to his expectations there was nothing solemn or beautiful about the entire exercise. To his utter amazement, the pious function was also the occasion of such sullied activities as beef eating :

> Even the most orthodox, it was said, ate beef because it
> Was cheeper, and some even risked their souls by relishing
> pork.
> The Sabbath was for betting and swearing and drinking.
>
> (*CP*, p. 235)

The Judaist in the poet felt upset how the demarcating line between the flesh and the spirit was demolished with the devouts devouring beef and others profaning their souls by tasting pork. The most unfortunate aspect of this marriage on the day of Sabbath was its defilement by betting and drinking, a day meant for religious asceticism. His being a liberal Jewish family there was nothing, however, much indecent and the couple was led to a studio for snaps. He reminisces how his honeymoon was celebrated on "a floor-mattress in the kitchen of my wife's family apartment." The poem closes on a hilarious note :

> During our first serious marriage quarrel she said Why did you take my virginity from me? I would gladly have returned it, but not one of the books I had read instructed me how.
>
> (*CP*, p. 235)

The piece "Song to be Shouted out" from the group of poems written for Ezekiel's nephew and Bombay-based popular singer

Nandu Bhende grapples with family discords. The wife assails the protagonist with infinite questions related to domestic chores :

> Did you post that letter?
> Did you make that telephone call?
> Did you pay that bill?
> What do you do all day?
>
> (*CP*, p. 241)

Though a member of patriarchal society, the poet presents himself as a victim of the fair sex, a perspective in keeping with his so-called anti-feminist stand. In all humility he accepts his *fait accompli* :

> It's good for my soul
> to be shouted at.
> Shout at me, woman!
> What else are wives for?
>
> (*CP*, p. 242)

The mutual infighting and brawl sickens the entire family including children and this is the burden of another piece titled "Family," another song for Nandu Bhende. The sense of disenchantment with life prompts the members to try ways and means to overcome the sense of defeat which has rendered this hallowed family institution into a virtual hell :

> Should we take to meditation
> transcendental, any other?
> Should we take to Zen?
> We cannot find our roots here,
> don't know where to go, Sir,
> don't know what to do, Sir,
> need a Guru, need a God.
> All of us are sick, Sir.
>
> (*CP*, p. 243)

Alarmed and unnerved, the victims search for Gurus like Sai Baba, Muktanand and Rajneesh under the illusion that their blessings might prove panacea for their ills. Ezekiel's denunciation of the so-called saints and religious preachers finds its still forceful expression in the poem "Healers." One can feel that a great admirer of W.H. Auden as Ezekiel is, he might mean by 'healers' the peers of Groddec, John Layard and Homer Lane, who showed the way out of existential impasse but they are otherwise. Since the death-wish has a huge toll, the fake "healers come in droves" and sell cures to umpteen clients looking helplessly at them. They make a roaring business by prescribing 'medicines' suited to the preferences of each patient :

> Sex is prohibited or allowed.
> Meat and drink are prohibited
> or allowed. Give up
> everything or nothing
> and be saved. The Master
> knows the secret.

(*CP*, p. 231)

Dealing with all sorts of people they acquire unique expertise in human psychology which strengthens them to beguile their clients. Creating an aura of superhuman or angelic attributes, they thrive on hypocrisy shamelessly :

> Know your *mantra*, meditate
> release your *kundalini*,
> get your *shakti* awakening
> and float with the spirit
> to your destination.

(*CP*, p. 232)

In his pursuit of the poetic idiom Ezekiel has liberally employed Indian words *mantra*, *kundalini*, *shakti* — to lend authenticity to the content.

The city life characterised by such destitute devotees and their fake saviours presents a confused picture of human activity. The poem "Hangover" provides impressionistic sketches of such life in a series of one-line vignettes where comment is made through sharp antithetical juxtapositions :

> The expensive menu and the shadow of Marx.
> The Biryani Hyderabadi and the sighs of Bangla Desh.
> The see-through dress and the show-nothing sari.
> The fog in the head and the sense of success
> The music Indian and the language English.

(*CP*, p. 232)

The references to places and concerns — Harbour Bar, Apollo Room, Taj, Churchgate, Borivli — show that this hangover is located in the contours of Bombay. The laconic title adds a new dimension to the piece as it conveys an involuntary awareness of a nightmarish situation. The satire, however, is softened in the closing stanza, made more inclusive by extension to the viewer himself. Devouring the sumptuous dish of Biryani Hyderabadi, an item in the expensive menu, while discussing Marx and his principles underlines the hypocrisy which typifies urban values.

From the protagonist's long walk to Churchgate carving a tenacious way between the pavement-sleepers, who constitute not an insubstantial bulk of the island population, one comes to Ezekiel's "Poverty Poem." The persona narrates the impressions of a foreign lady who was moved to pity at the sight of a beggar boy, almost naked, alone, and slightly bent and parted with some coins. The boy probably expressed his sense of joy by smiling at the foreigner which she reciprocated without decoding his gestures full well :

> 'Before he released me,
> he smiled and I smiled back,
> I turned and gave him a coin,
> past belief in that or anything.'
> She didn't know beggars in India
> smile only at white foreigners.

(*CP*, pp. 230-231)

Ezekiel's dig at the typical trait of Indian beggars who "smile only at white foreigners," has been frowned upon by many a critic. It has been argued that Ezekiel's non-native ancestry surfaces at places in his debunking of Indian phenomena. Reading in between the lines, one feels Ezekiel is articulating his own impressions in that the colour of his skin also resembles the 'white foreigners.' G.N. Devy complains of lack of "self transforming emotion"[1] in the poem. While appreciating this piece for "the valued qualities of irony and ambivalence," the noted critic calls it 'tamasik' poetry in Aurobindo-terminology because it is "neither interesting to man, nor pleasing to gods." To use the Aurobindo stick to beat Ezekiel with appears hardly fair and justified in that Ezekiel has his own poetic creed and his diatribe against Aurobindo is part of the historical development of modern Indian poetry in English.

Ezekiel as a humanist feels that human values necessarily forge ties between individuals while language serves as a hurdle in this process. In "Minority Poem," haunted by 'invisible guests' in his room, the poet engages himself in a dialogue with them obviously to explain his standpoint to the extent of exhaustion. The limitations of human language prompt him to ponder deeper over this phenomenon and he ultimately realises that human values unite, while language reverses the process :

> It's the language really
> separates, whatever else
> is shared. On the other hand,
> Everyone understands
> Mother Teresa; her guests
> die visibly in her arms.
>
> (*CP*, p. 236)

The image recalls Michael angelo's Pieta. The comparison of Mother Teressa with the Virgin Mary becomes more meaningful if one views the "Annunciation" to symbolise Mary's acceptance of her duty as mother, the creator and protector. In his extremely revealing essay, "Parables and Commonplaces," A.K. Ramanujan voices similar sentiments :

> ... the encounters begin with emphasis on differences, and end in a moment of communication below the threshold of language — often a recognition of the body's universalities, whether it is pregnancy and birth, or a mother's death and a son's mourning, a recognition of oneness, however momentary.[2]

In his humanist phase Ezekiel is obviously preoccupied with perennial values which defy barriers and discriminations. The concluding stanza emphasises that linguistic and technical expertise is of no avail "While the city burns." The poem argues that the selfish inhabitants of the city have thrown all human values to winds and they are busy in cut-throat competitions driven by temporal concerns. Unless there is a change of heart, external apparatuses are pitiably deficient to remedy the situation and make it reasonably worth-living.

The piece "Credo' from "Postcard Poems" centres in the complexity of human life which can be sustained only "by the human need/to hear new messages." It begins with the central artistic concern :

> To know beneath
> the depth of life
> another depth begin;
> blindly to sink...
>
> (*CP*, p. 244)

The intriguing human predicament underlines the limits of creative effort to reach at it and the closer one seems, the further one moves. While ruminating over his art and its salutary impact Ezekiel compares himself inadvantageously with Wordsworth in "Dilemma" :

> Should I be surprised :
> trader in paradoxes,
> ally of the dialectic?
> I shake with intimations —
> not of immortality .
>
> (*CP*, p. 244)

The opening poem of *Latter-Day Psalms* "Counsel," is a brief summing up of the experiences of life which are despairing rather than encouraging. The title "Counsel" conveys a deeper sense of involvement than a casual word 'advice' might have done. It is only appropriate to old age that the poet of 'Barbaric city sick with slums' has been able to overcome his earlier disenchantment and has learnt to live in sickness and slums. Palpably in an endearing mood he wishes to pass on the encapsulated wisdom to the next generation. The protagonist plays down success, so ardently sought for by people and rarely achieved — "success at thc moment/Is not in your interest." Sounding like a fatalist the poet suggests :

> Turn to silence, nothingness.
> Where you are
> Is where you have to be.
>
> (*CP*, p. 229)

He further advises to identify personal weaknesses as part of human existence and thus to enrich and strengthen one's personality.

Knowing full well that this is a difficult proposition, the persona emphasizes :

> Know, you are not wise :
> This is difficult.
> Grasp your folly
>
> And grasp yourself.

(*CP*, p. 229)

The overriding caution — "Do without, be absent" — to exist within limitations and imperfections has some tinge of material condemnation which is unfortunately treated by people as the *summum bonum* of life. Written under the natural impact of "Hymns in Darkness," the poem's central burden is to celebrate life in all its folly and to imbibe a helping and sacrificing attitude towards others :

> Express your gratitude
> By giving what you have to give.
> You may get nothing in return.
>
> And bear your restlessness with grace.

(*CP*, p. 230)

This single line coda pleads for putting up with the strife-torn life with grace becoming one created in the image of God.

In the poem "At 62," the poet seems to present his credentials which amply qualify him for being a counsel to future generations. With the passage of time and the dawning of old age, the poet visualizes something approaching which is most dismal — "Death/ in the distance/ and near,/ is my only halo." In the face of an enemy as indefatigable as death the poet plans to offer a modest resistance through experiences which rendered life a meaning and purpose. Still absorbed in 'the ordinariness of events,' Ezekiel even at the ripe old age of 62 does feel that the familiar human drama is not less engaging for being ordinary :

> I celebrate the familiar,
> the routine,
> and the unexpected.

(*CP*, p. 273)

Old age has vouchsafed upon him an enlargement of self which has enabled him to think of others while thinking of himself. The concluding stanza very poignantly communicates the pathos of temporal existence :

> I want my hands
> to learn how to heal
> myself and others,
> before I hear
> my last song.

(*CP*, p. 274)

The apprehension of the inevitable — "before I hear/my last song" — finds a more poignant expression in the poem "A Different Way." The protagonist is at his wits' end to mark the dichotomies of life which defy spiritual trainings and accomplishments. He fails to experience for himself the real meditative peace in his resounding silences and also the mystical stillness in his mundane movements. The theoretical aspects simply cannot cope with the practicalities of life characterised by dull monotony, sensuality and the nefarious parade of the self. The following lines border on self pity and any mortal can see his image mirrored in the protagonist :

> Now I feel driven to the wall
> by age and circumstance :
> holiness matters.

(*CP*, p. 272)

Even in the face of such a pathetic predicament, the protagonist's unrelenting hatred against mushroom growth of saints and gurus restrains him from seeking solace by visiting an ashram. Tired of experimenting with the conservative spiritual remedies, he outlines a different programme :

> I have begun to imagine
> a different way
> in which things become holy
> as they remain the same.

(*CP*, p. 272)

The poem does not celebrate "difference" unless it be the difference of knowing that humanity must, if one may borrow a business metaphor in this age of inexorable capitalism, invest in a common fund. In an earlier poem "Transmutation" Ezekiel had observed :

> Do not, in your vanity, the tenuous thread
> of difference flaunt, but be
> Asserted in the common dance.

(*CP*, p. 56)

The poem "Blessings" is Blakean in spirit, a mystique of the ordinary, with the poet offering his heartiest wishes to the readers, for their peace and well being. Comprising fourteen sections, these blessings centre round common human experiences one is prone to be unmindful of on one count or the other. A significant feature of this piece is its epigrammatic, ironic and proverbial character with intermittent touches of word play and puns. The opening 'blessing' wishes for a balanced attitude to life, not blinded by vague opinions. There is a subtle hint to look for divine in the ordinary, "May you read wisdom books/in the spirit of the comics" and *vice versa*. The general human concern prompts the poet to wish for his casual readers an instinctive awareness as to the slightest loss of natural resources like water leakage from taps even though they are not directly affected by it. The apparent humorous touch aids to the intended effect. The third 'blessing' prays to the Almighty for the cognitive awareness of his fellow beings as it would bring about a qualitative improvement in their intrinsic individual selves. This might enable them to overcome the dark abyss which is their *fait accompli* :

> Be drunk, occasionally,
> but not with gin
> or whisky. May the Lord
> use you up for ends
> beyond your means,
> so you know what drunkenness
> really means.

(*CP*, p. 280)

Man is involuntarily involved in the pursuit of happiness which more often than not turns out to be a mirage. The crux of the fourth venediction is the capability to realise happiness in each and every human activity if discharged tastefully. The prayer which follows it is the core of "Blessings" :

Whenever you worship
the Absolute,
may you remember
all its Relatives.

(*CP*, p. 281)

The above excerpt dwells on the perennial dichotomy between the absolute and the relative, which are invariably treated as poles apart. However, the blesser here has a much broader vision and cannot think of the one in a complete absence of the other. The overtly humanistic concern is betrayed in the poet's wish that the worship of God should not be done in isolation from the other creatures created by Him. Remembering 'all its Relatives' implies that the human vision must include the whole of the Universe in its ken.

The sixth blessing lays emphasis on the importance of time for one who leads a time-bound existence, while the seventh one underlines the importance of humility, a virtue frequently sought after but rarely achieved. The prayer that follows it underscores the necessity of making the most of life granted to man. Whether in solitude or in company, this joy for life can make it all the more desirable and meaningful. In the ninth section, the poet prays to the Almighty to bless his readers with consolation in their moments of utmost tension and frustration, the very trying moments when one fails to decode any meaning in mundane existence. In the tenth blessing, the poet pleads for the value of warmth for life which can render religion, mundane experiences and convictions great purpose and significance.

The humanist in Ezekiel is endowed with extensive vista and his concerns are not confined simply to homo-sapiens. Flora and Fauna of the universe coexist and have their meaning in togetherness. Should circumstances deprive him of real natural surroundings, he may have the imaginative strength to create his own trees because 'one impulse from a vernal wood may teach' him to live and love in the lap of nature. The couple of blessings that follow grapple with the reader's responsibility to his age and the paradigms to conduct himself in it. The concluding blessing is for the readers who comprise Noah's Arc :

May you be
poet, painter, scholar
thinker, musician,
even if you create nothing that matters
except your life, which too
has to be created.

(*CP*, p. 283)

Irrespective of one's profession or the intellectual stature, each individual's life is a self-creation, one is what one makes of oneself.

It is worth noting that these blessings are so vast and enormous that they encompass the whole of humanity. This Ezekiel is far different from his earlier self who had been worried about finding his own salvation — "All I want now/is the recognition/of dilemma/ and the quickest means/of resolving it/within my limits" ("Transparently," p. 150). These blessings testify that the poet has made himself one with the hoary tradition of India characterized by a pervasive involvement.

"Latter-Day Psalms" represents the summit of Ezekiel's spiritual speculations though he has denied times without number that he is not a religious poet in the accepted sense of the term. In a letter to V.A. Shahane, he wrote :

> I am not a religious or even a moral person in any conventional sense. Yet, I have always felt myself to be religious and moral in some sense. The gap between these two statements is the existential sphere of my poetry.[3]

The space between religious conviction and an atheistic enquiry is no-man's land and Ezekiel's choice to inhabit it is quite suggestive. The following description of the circumstances behind the composition of "Latter-Day Psalms" demonstrates that it was not a sudden eruption of some revelation :

> It was the total silence of my hotel room (at Rotterdam where Ezekiel had gone to do a poetry reading from 11-17 June 1978) that made me want to write. I had no reading material with me, but there was a copy of the Gideon Bible beside my bed. I read some of my

> favourite passages from Jonah and Job, then turned to the psalms. I've had a special relationship with them since the age of twelve, a dissenting relationship which have been suppressed, feelings stretching over 40 years suddenly crystalised. Before leaving Rotterdam I had completed nine "Latter-Day Psalms," the tenth and concluding one being written in Berlin.[4]

The modifier "Lattter-Day" in the title underlines the irrelevance of the Biblical Psalms to contemporary consciousness which is pathetically concerned with the immediate and the real and as such these old Psalms need to be retouched and appropriated so that a compromise formula could be evolved to seek God. From a strictly religious angle such a proposition is highly blasphemous and amounts to insulting God. The latter-day psalmist is obviously more rational, pragmatic and conscious of the metaphoric weakness of the liturgical piece. Ezekiel himself intended these psalms to be "only Post-Judaic-Christian."[5] The first nine psalms correspond to 9 of the 150 Old Testament Psalms. They set off echoing an identical language and imagery but soon Ezekiel achieves ironic effects recasting their original sense in such a way as to overturn their meaning.

The comparison of Ezekiel's first psalm with its Biblical counterpart is imperative to underscore the quality of adaptation which informs this group of poems. Psalm I begins thus :

> Blessed is the man that walketh not in the Counsel of the ungodly, nor standeth in the way of sinners, nor sitteth in the seat of the scornful. But his delight is in the Law of the Lord; and in this law doth he meditate day and night.[6]

The first latter-day psalm verbally objectifies the humanistic outlook :

> Blessed is the man that walketh
> not in the counsel of the conventional,
> and is at home with
> sin as with a wife. He shall
> listen patiently to the scornful,
> and understand the sources of their scorn.

> He does not meditate day and night on
> anything; his delight
> is in action.
>
> (*CP*, p. 252)

The outrageous analogy "at home with/sin as with a wife" affirms the world of experience. It argues that the enjoyment of sin is a means towards tolerance, understanding and salvation. The poet advocates involvement in life, an admixture of both good and evil and not to be frightened by confrontation with "the ungodly." Almost voicing the Gandhian philosophy of 'hate the sin and not the sinner,' he is willing to sympathise with the depraved by acquainting himself with their miserable situation. The Biblical advice to avoid the reprobate lacks human element because man was made in the 'image of God.' The plan to defy the accepted religious values has a humane logic behind it. The utilitarian mind of the modern man cannot afford the luxury of an outright submission even to the "Law of the Lord."

The second verse alludes to the *Gita*'s doctrine of dispassionate action or work without any involvement with the outcome. It puts to logic this philosophy because man lives in time and "Rare is the man whose fruit is/in his season." With 'the Time's chariot drawing near,' the poet pleads that to look for a positive conclusion is an irresistible temptation. Ironically enough the good are not any better off than the evil inasmuch as both have a temporal existence. This congregation of the righteous and the wrongful is a motley of mortals suffering their terms of punishment.

Ezekiel's second psalm is modelled after the third Psalm with reverberating echoes of Hinduism in its catholic approach. The opening verse prays to God for saving both the evil and the good from their potential human weaknesses. The Biblical Psalm 3 ends thus :

> Arise, O Lord : save me, O my God; for thou hast
> smitten all mine enemies upon the cheekbone; thou
> hast broken the teeth of the ungodly.
>
> Salvation belongeth unto the Lord : thy
> blessing is upon thy people.

In his psalm the poet creates his characteristic humour by taking the literal import of "Thou hast broken the teeth of the ungodly" :

> How can I breathe freely if
> thou breakest the teeth of
> the ungodly?

(*CP*, p. 254)

Ezekiel is more tolerant, more permissive and broad minded than the Biblical psalmist. He reaches out to the whole of mankind, not only to those who belong to a particular church. The humanity of the above extract contrasts sharply with the vengeful conceit of its original counterpart.

The third latter-day psalm parodies Eighth Psalm which declares, "Thou madest him to have dominion over the work of thy hands." Ezekiel's appropriation betrays a direct criticism of modern life and civilisation which has wrought great havoc on natural habitat and environmental balance :

> What have we done with the dominion
> thou hast given us? What are we
> doing to the sheep and the oxen and the
> beasts of the field, the fowl of the
> air and the fish of the sea?

(*CP*. p. 255)

In the fourth Latter-Day Psalm, the inquisitive spirit of Ezekiel questions the faith of David about God being the protector of all creatures as reflected in Psalm 23 :

> The Lord is my shepherd;
> I shall not want.
> He makes me to lie down in green pastures;
> He leads me beside the still waters.

He is not willing to be convinced that under His care, he can experience perfection and wantlessness. As to the green pastures, he wishes to be led from idleness to work which could be shepherding one's own self. In respect of the conviction — "I will fear no evil" — Ezekiel says :

> When my soul is restored,
> I walk the path of self-
> righteousness.

I do fear evil : Thy rod
and thy staff do comfort
me.

Let not my table be prepared
in the presence of anybody.
I do not need a cup that
runneth over.

(*CP*, p. 255)

The ardent wish to follow the path of self-righteousness (not righteousness) bespeaks Ezekiel's faith in human dignity which he never puts on stake. Keeping the human predicament in mind, the poet takes nothing for granted for ever, not even the assets that accrue to the faithful by the Lord's grace.

The fifth latter-day psalm begins with Ezekiel's reflection on Jewish diaspora and the fragmentation of a well-knit community throughout the world. It alludes to Psalm 60 :

O God, You have cast us off,
You have broken us down;
You have been displeased;
Oh, restore us again!

The gripping anxiety transforms itself into an impelling urge — "Where shall/we live in peace with our/neighbours?" The misery of the Semites did not end up with their exodus from Israel — "The end is not yet" — and much more suffering seems to be in store for the Jews. The religious fanaticism overrides all other considerations and insanity becomes the guiding principle. The indiscriminate genocide of the Jews in Nazi Germany is alarmingly imprinted in the poet's psyche :

Vain is the help of man,
and vain everything else.
Did none pray who was ca-
ught in the Holocaust?

It is nowhere, said by King
David that God is on the
side of the big battalions.

> Philistia triumphs because of thee
> or, by an irony, over thee.
>
> (*CP*, p. 256)

The breaking up of the word 'caught' in two lines "ca-/ught" indicates a choked voice to reminisce the wholesale loss of lives. Engaging himself in a friendly conversation, as it were, Ezekiel alludes to the Psalms of David which never sang that He sides with the strong and oppressive. The poet charges Him with encouraging uncultured people who ironically falsify the very values dear to His heart. The Psalmist says, "Though God, we will do valiantly,/For it is He who shall tread down our enemies." The poet is at his wit's end to see that his enemies are equally enthusiastic much less discouraged because God seems to be disinclined to tread down them — "We do valiantly, and so do/our enemies."

Derived from Psalm 78, the sixth section dwells on "the testimony in Jacob" blatantly "refused by/the rebellious generation of/the times." The contradiction between theory and practice has become staringly pronounced. The German mishap has a more direct reference here. There is an implicit reference also to the following lines of Psalm 31 :

> Blessed be the Lord,
> For He has shown me His marvellous kindness in a
> strong city!

The poet puts up the question :

> How long are we to rely
> on those marvellous things
> in ancient Egypt? Tell me of the
> marvellous things in Nazi Germany.
> Even with manna in our mouths,
> we are not estranged from our lust.
>
> (*CP*, p. 257)

The employment of the adjective 'marvellous' twice in the above passage suggests Ezekiel's impatience with the talk of all miraculous and charismatic activities associated with the Christ. Its use in two different contexts, "ancient Egypt" and "Nazi Germany" underlines the contrast between the two situations and immensely adds to the ironic effect. The recent happenings in human history, particularly during the inter-War years, the poet feels, underscore the typical human depravity for power and prestige. He finds fault with the Psalmist who was unmindful of human vulnerability to obey God's command.

It is against this background that Ezekiel's seventh psalm opens up with a strong case for reviewing the Book of Psalms afresh. It is designed after Psalm 95 which begins thus :

Oh come, let us sing to the Lord!
Let us shout joyfully to the Rock of our salvation
Let us come before His presence with thanksgiving;
Let us shout joyfully to Him with Psalms.

Ezekiel's psalm opens as follows :

Come, let us make a joyful no-
ise unto him with psalms.

And a different noise with
Latter-Day Psalms.

(*CP*, p. 258)

Irony in the first couple of lines derives from a pointed use of an unorthodox punctuation subtly indicative of a spirit of denigration and deliberate breaking of the word 'noise.' The lower-case lettering in respect of 'H' and 'P' in the second line subverts, rather invalidates, the Psalm's meanings. The justification for a new set of devotional psalms spells the fate of institutionalised religion in an agnostic age. The Psalms after Psalms glorify macrocosm, its flora and fauna, created by the Lord. The modern poet is sometimes unfavourably disposed to look at them :

The sea is his; we may drown
in it. He formed the dry land,
on which many millions thirst
to no end.

(*CP*, p. 258)

An almost identical denigration of the sublime to the ludicrous occurs in A.K. Ramanujan's well-known piece "Prayers to Lord Murugan" :

Lord of solutions,
teach us to dissolve
and not to drown.

(*The Collected Poems of A.K. Ramanujan*, p. 119)

Times without number the Psalms hammer on the consciousness that 'the Lord is my Shepherd' who owns green pastures. Ezekiel toys with the literal meaning of these words to ridicule the original context impregnated with deep symbolic undertones. The ambiguous associations of 'sheep' are exploited in the following passage to deflate the Psalmist's chauvinistic self-righteousness which reads like a nursery-rhyme :

We are the people of his pa-
sture, we are the sheep
of his hand. Baa Baa Black Sheep.

(*CP*, p. 258)

Equating hymns to nonsense verse smacks of an erratic secular thinking even to a common man with no religious credentials. The poet feels sorry for the misplaced religious zeal of the forefathers in singing the glory of God.

Ezekiel's eighth psalm is extensively based on the Psalm 102 where the afflicted devotee complains before the Lord about his temporal existence. He compares himself with other creatures of the universe :

I am like a pelican of the wilderness;
I am like an owl of the desert.
I lie away,
And am like a sparrow alone on the housetop.

Ezekiel's song opens verbatim only with subtle modifications :

I am like a pelican of the wild-
erness, like an owl of the de-
sert, like a sparrow alone
upon the housetop — but not in
misery.

I forget to eat my bread,
not because my heart is
withered like grass.

(*CP*, p. 259)

While mortality has obliterated the Psalmist's every other consideration, including the bare necessities like food to survive, the poet regrets to 'eat his bread' due to entirely different reasons. The two psalmists have a common point, however, to worship God who "regards/the prayer of the destitute, who hears the groanings of the/prisoner, and of those who are/appointed to death." The humble anguish of the Biblical singer over this appointment with death makes him cry :

> They will perish, but you will endure;
> yes, all of them will grow old like a garment;
> Like a cloak you will change them,
> And they will be changed....
> The children of Your servants will continue,
> And their descendants will be established before You.

Ezekiel simply borrows the metonymy in his psalm with no complaints as to his predicament :

> I wax old as a garment;
> as a vesture I am changed.
> In this I accept the condition of humanity.
>
> My children shall continue,
> and their children shall
> continue...

(*CP*, p. 259)

As has been noted in the preceding chapter, Ezekiel had acquired a sound grounding in the Hindu scriptures and in the above extract there are eloquent echoes of Lord Krishna's celebrated advice to Arjuna :

> Vāsānsi jīrnāni yathā vihāya, navāni grihnāti naroparāni.
> Tathā sharirāni vihāya jīrna, nyānyani sanyāti navāni dehī.

The agony of the time-bound human phenomenon has been upsetting man ever since Adam's Fall. In his illustrious poem "Ode to a Nightingale" John Keats refers to this situation :

> Thou wast not born for death, immortal bird!
> No hungry generations tread thee down.

Even W.B. Yeats's central preoccupation has been human mutability so eloquently voiced in the well-known line "Those dying generations." That this temporariness has come to stay with man has been perceptively indicated by Ezekiel with three dots as if this endless occurrence were baffling to be put into words.

The penultimate "Latter-Day Psalm" overhauls Psalm 127 which is Solomon's song, a Song of Ascents. The original reads as follows :

> Unless the Lord builds the house,
> They labour in vain who build it;...
> It is vain for you to rise up early,
> To sit up late,
> To eat the bread of sorrows;...

Unlike the Psalmist who derives the symbolic meaning of 'building the house,' Ezekiel takes its literal one to reduce the gravity of the context :

> Except the Lord build the ho-
> use — and not even always then —
> they labour in vain that build
> it. Yet, it is better to build
> than to abstain from building,
> and no labour is altogether
> in vain
> It is not vain to rise
> up early, to sit up late,
> to eat the bread of sorrow.

(*CP*, p. 260)

Ezekiel argues like a common man that doing something is infinitely better than being allergic to work culture. As a humanist he opines that no labour, howsoever apparently unrewarding, is entirely wasted as they say, 'Failures are the pillars of success.' One also recalls Ezekiel's early resolve — "Let me not be isolated/Uninvolved in Man's defeat" (p. 56) — in this context. In another context T.S. Eliot once said, "It is better to do evil than nothing, at least we exist." Ezekiel achieves humorous effect in his poetry by employing several strategies, pronounced among them being an oblique reference to some well-known maxim or statement. Trifling with the literal import of 'rise' and 'sit,' he rejects part of the Psalmist's eulogy and the reader enjoys this toying up calling to mind the everyday counsel, 'Early to bed and early to rise, makes a man healthy, wealthy and wise.' He further appropriates the later part of the Psalm :

> Behold, children are a heritage from the Lord,...
> Like arrows in the hand of a warrior,...
> Happy is the man who has his quiver full of them;...

to suit the contemporary Indian context of family planning :

> Children are as arrows in
> the hands of a mighty man,
> but not everyman is mighty.
> Lo, children are an heritage
> of the Lord, but a quiver
> full of them is not ess-
> ential for happiness.

(*CP*, p. 260)

Being blessed with hosts of children has nothing to pride on particularly in view of the Malthusian spectre.

The tenth piece titled "Concluding Latter-Day Psalm" is a "comment on the previous nine as well as on the 150 Old Testament Psalms" ("An Indian Poet in Rotterdam"). While the last Biblical Psalm, *i.e.*, Psalm 150 enjoins upon the reader to "Praise the Lord" for His mighty acts, Ezekiel dismisses its content as "All that fuss about faith." He finds the make-believe world of ritualistic verbosity and high sounding declarations unbearably trying and deplorable :

> How boring and pathetic, but
> also how elemental, how spiritual
> the language, how fiery and human
> in the folly of its feelings!

(*CP*, p. 260)

This modest assessment of Psalms borders on eccentricity for a man of religious convictions. One may differ from his conclusions which include a significant comment — "how fiery and human/in the folly of its feelings" — from the perspective of this study. It has been the present researcher's contention throughout that Ezekiel is basically a humanist endowed with an instinctive empathy for man's weaknesses. Despite questioning the sincerity of the Psalmist's feelings, he admires them because they are human creations, destined to be flawed and incomplete. Commenting on the poetic virtues of the Psalms, he admires also their lyrical quality and the richness of images, and avers, "they swim in my Jewish consciousness." Reciting these Psalms as a precocious child of an orthodox Jewish family from the very early years, a time much before the domain of experience, the poet admits their instinctive awareness in the making of his sensibility. This long sequence of poems concludes with the following lines where the poet reiterates the significance of Biblical Psalms in the growth of his personality :

> The images are beautiful words
> and colourful fish : they fly,
> they swim in my Jewish consciousness....
> Now I am through with
> the Psalms; they are
> part of my flesh.
>
> (*CP*, p. 261)

Even in an interview with Dharkers in 1979, within a year of the completion of the poem Ezekiel honestly admitted :

> I think the problem of identity is important in all literary and cultural activity. I don't believe its possible to be a universal man without some specific roots which are strengthened, accepted or revolted against ... Of late I've found myself more deliberately turning to Jewish sources and themes as though some inner movement has required it.[7]

Ezekiel's non-conformist response to Psalms ingrained in the catholicity of human love, however, lacks spiritual ambience but its emperical character makes it more engaging and thought provoking. Bruce King tellingly observes :

> The 'Latter-Day Psalms' demolish claims by those in authority to know the good from the bad, to be just or to represent the divine... The 'Latter-Day Psalms' reflect Ezekiel's struggle with his own Jewish heritage and end with an ironic 'Jamini Roy' conclusion in which the art of the Psalms provides a model for his own work.[8]

Ezekiel assumes the role of a prophet though in a humorous vein in the "Edinburgh Interlude" written for Edinburgh Festival of the Arts, 1983. In its XXVII section titled "Prophet," he says, "I ask the prophet in me/ to say where I must go next." The primary meaning of a prophet like Moses or Christ is not intended here but their authority for the command of truth is transferred to the context to indicate the authority of his conscience. In a spirit of stocktaking of his earlier anxieties and frustrations, the poet muses :

> The prophet in me
> recovered from his despair.
> Let me open your old wounds, he said,
> your suffering
> may help you find the place
> Where you need to be.
>
> (*CP*, p. 294)

The opening up of old wounds and the suffering involved in it recalls to mind Ezekiel's sensitivity to human suffering even as a small boy. In his famous poem "Night of the Scorpion" the poet remembers how the villagers prayed for the quick relief of his scorpion-stung mother :

> May your suffering decrease
> the misfortunes of your next birth, they said.
>
> (*CP*, p. 130)

Suffering purifies flesh of its sins and as such is not that undesirable. The image of Cross has been ironically employed in Section IV of "Ten Poems of the Greek Anthology Mode" :

> Asked about his critics,
> The poet moaned : They crucify me
> Because I am creative.
> Asked about a contemporary,
> Sometimes admired, he played iconoclast
> And howled
> 'He's is not a major poet by any standards.'
> Then he crawled back proudly to his Cross.
>
> (*CP*, p. 274)

This alacrity to accept Cross is a human attribute and in one of his major interviews, Ezekiel refers to the essence of his personality, "I would prefer to claim that nine times out of ten my being human is more important than anything else in the whole world" (*Selected Prose*, p. 173). A discreet perusal of his poetry shows that such a claim is perfectly justified. In one of his earliest poems "A Time to Change," he expresses his determination to value even traditional tools by human parametres — "but I am human/And must justify to what they mean" (*CP*, p. 5). In another poem "The Double Horror" he bemoans human degradation — "Reduced to something less than human by the crowd" (CP, p. 7). In one of his "Uncertain Certainties" Ezekiel says, "No oasis in our spiritual desert is more welcome than a human being who actually grants us our full human reality" (*Selected Prose*, p. 128). 'Granting full human reality' implies awareness of human frailty and limitations, the littleness or smallness of man which has innate potentiality to withstand adversity. In the XIII, "Hymns in Darkness" which is explicitly autobiographical, the persona tells about the poet as :

> A tireless social human being
> destined always
> to know defeat
> like a twin brother.
>
> (*CP*, p. 223)

The astute knowledge that failure and man are twins, underlines the peculiarity of human situation which can be redeemed by this realisation alone. Confiding to his biographer R. Raj Rao in a half humorous vein, Ezekiel said that he would title his autobiography "A Thousand Failures" if he ever wrote one (*Nissim Ezekiel : The Authorized Biography*, p. 24). No wonder if the poet works out a fitting epitaph for himself :

> Here lies a poet whose theme was human failure
> For which he was praised in a dozen famous obituaries.
>
> (*CP*, p. 275)

'Human failure' has ever been Ezekiel's central motif and the poems written in the last phase beginning since 1976 are simply a reiteration, an unequivocal expression of his humanistic preoccupations. The poetic odyssey that started with a set of intermittent passionate urges culminated in the confirmation of perennial human values that cut across ethnic, racial and geographical boundaries in his recent poetic phase.

REFERENCES

1. G.N. Devy, "A Theory, for Instance," *In Another Tongue* (Madras : Macmillan, 1993), p. 61.
2. A.K. Ramanujan, "Parables and Commonplaces" in Amirthanayagam, Guy, (ed.), *Writers in East-West Encounter : New Cultural Bearins* (London : Macmillan, 1982), p.145.
3. V.A. Shahane, "The Religious-Philosophical Strain in Nissim Ezekiel's Poetry," *Journal of South Asian Literature*, 11, 3-4 (Spring-Summer, 1976), 261.
4. Malvika R. Khanna, "An Indian Poet in Rotterdam," *The Times of India*, 17 August 1978, 13.
5. Shyamala A. Narayan, Nissim Ezekiel's *Latter-Day Psalms* : A Study, *Journal of Indian Writing in English*, 13, 1 (Jan. 1985), 36.
6. All Biblical Psalms are quoted from King James's *Authorised Version of the Bible.*
7. Imtiaz and Anil Dharker, "Interview : Nissim Ezekiel," *Indian Literary Review*, 1, 10 (Feb. 1979), 2-8.
8. *Three Indian Poets*, (New Delhi : Oxford, 1991), p. 48.

6

The Final Estimate

Nissim Ezekiel began his poetic journey gripped by a host of inhibitive complexes owing to his Jewish background. The instinctive awareness of marginality is primarily responsible for the recurring notes of anguish and anxiety in his poetry which records his incessant struggle to transcend his position and force himself onto the centre. The impelling urge of the marginal to meet the mighty prompted Ezekiel to formulate personal strategies to devise his relevance to his surroundings. He began with developing a sense of commitment and belonging, to broaden his individual self in his creative pilgrimage and this concern is most pervasively pronounced in his poetic universe.

The poetic odyssey that started with a set of challenges and conflicts was further aggravated by his choice of English as the poetic medium instead of going in for some Indian languages. The critics have invariably employed the word 'alienation' to describe his situation and more often than not this has been treated as an inherent and in-built handicap for a proper appreciation of the native scenario. To be fair to him, a proper evaluation of his poetic achievement must take into account his literary presumptions and predilections. In his writings, poems, interviews and Radio talks he has made no secret of his identification only with Modern India and not with the historical and cultural past of the country. Endowed with an extremely critical temperament he has uninhibitedly questioned the existing conventions and mannerisms and has directed some of his sharpest queries at the smugness of contemporary Indian life. In his persistent interrogations and quarrels with the prevailing notions of culture, he betrays an Eliot-like cultural obsession. If Eliot tried to define culture in Christian terms and talked of the mind of Europe to ensure his acceptance in the English tradition, Ezekiel pleaded for broadening the scope of culture :

> I am against a monolithic culture in a totalitarian society, but the alternative is not an indifferent, sterile culture or conglomeration of cultures, each steeped in its hopelessly stagnant ideas. The alternative is a critical spirit which will bring culture alive, making old ideas new and new ideas sound (*Selected Prose*, p. 74).

The present intensive study of his poetry undertaken in three well-marked phases in the preceding pages has underscored the significant milestones of his creative journey. Ezekiel's romantic poetry centres round perennial romantic themes of love, nature, loneliness and transience. The obsessive awareness of human frailty coupled with a casual urge to transcend it creates a tension which the poet attempts to cover up by a frequent use of irony as a self defensive weapon. In the absence of a great personal crisis on emotional plane, like the failure of the French Revolution in the case of Wordsworth, all that Ezekiel could do was to undergo a process of rigorous self-scrutiny bordering on confessional mode. To label specific traits in terms of systems of belief is a common tendency with scholars and Ezekiel's poetry has been exhaustively analysed from this angle. Critics after critics from V.A. Shahane to P.K.J. Kurup have ingeniously tried to accommodate him in one philosophic system or the other. However, a dispassionate examination of poems demonstrates that Ezekiel defies philosophical categorisation whatsoever. He has neither rigidly followed any philosophy nor meticulously endeavoured to build up one for himself. An astute study of the critical scholarship on Ezekiel evidences that his spiritual concerns have been mistaken for implicit religious certitude. The exigesis of his poetry in religious terms is apparently far-fetched and the height of erroneous criticism is reached when his poems are found lacking in devotional spirit of the English metaphysical poets of the seventeenth century.

Nissim Ezekiel's vociferous declarations about his involvement with Indian scene fail to convince a discerning reader of his poetry. A conspicuous absence of poems arousing patriotic zeal or those envisaging the future of an emancipating India, significantly attests to his peripheral concerns with the native scenario. What Bruce King regards as his greatest strength — "untempted by the nationalist sentiments" (*Three Indian Poets*, p. 20) — eventually turns out to be Ezekiel's weakness. Perceptive as the poet is, he could anticipate unfavourable response to his experiences and wrote : ... "I love India, I expect nothing in return because critical, sceptical love does not beget love" (*Selected Prose*, p. 99). In defence of Ezekiel, it can be argued that the post-Independence nationalism needs be slightly refined, ironic and critical as compared to that of the colonial times. It is a nationalism of no mean quality to expose with an unusual detachment the corruption infecting the Indian polity. Ezekiel's laconic observations in poems like "Truth about the Floods" and "In India," are too telling to be easily forgotten, founded as they are in real situations.

Cultural anguish and anxiety which inform a large number of Ezekiel's early poems finally yield to an unusual sense of acceptance and affirmation suggesting that the poet has cast off his initial prejudices and apprehensions. By coming to terms with his surroundings the angry individualist in Ezekiel acquires a serenity that inevitably endows him with an enlarged imaginative sympathy. The odyssey from *A Time to Change* to the latest *Edinburgh Interlude* has milestones like *The Unfinished Man*, *The Exact Name* and *Hymns in Darkness*. The final affirmation comes when the earlier proposition of sticking to "My backward place is where I am" achieves a bolder tone "to suffer in one's own hell." With this ushered in a phase of unusual celebration of "the familiar/the routine/and the unexpected" and "driven to the wall/by age and circumstance," the poet realises that ultimately holiness matters. The old age has conferred upon him an enlargement of self which has enabled him to think of others while thinking of himself :

I want my hands
to learn how to heal
myself and others,
before I hear
my last song.

(*CP*, p. 274)

Ezekiel's poetic canvas is much wider and his thematic concerns far subsuming than those of other contemporary poets. If R. Parthasarathy ceaselessly harps on his Tamil roots and Jayant Mahapatra is busy reinvigorating Oriya cultural past, Ezekiel is not even distantly nostalgic about his Jewish homeland. While Kamala Das is obsessively preoccupied with defining self in terms of her personal experiences, A.K. Ramanujan picks up the 'family metaphor' to relate himself to South-Indian Brahmanic tradition, the crux of Ezekiel's poetic absorption is to find his relevance in terms of the surrounding reality. Armed with an ironic vision and an unusual sense of humour, Ezekiel's technical accomplishments lend his poetry a uniqueness which can be matched neither by Kamala Das's sentimental outpourings nor by Ramanujan's cross-cultural predilections.

Nissim Ezekiel's contribution to Modern Indian poetry in English lies among other things, in his modernising its idiom. Besides bringing out eight volumes of poems, he has extensively lectured on poetry, art and culture. He has been the poetic mentor of about a dozen major Indian poets who have immensely benefited from his encouragement, advice and guidance. The post-colonial Indian poetry in English owes much to him because his ideas, attitudes and perceptions of life have become almost synonymous with the plurality of the Indian ethos. If Auden was looked upon by his contemporaries as the poetic messiah who showed them the way out of the Waste Land, Ezekiel can be rightly estimated with a similar praise in respect of post-Independence poetic scene which was hopelessly chaotic at the time of his emergence.

Select Bibliography

PRIMARY SOURCES

(i) Poetical Works

A Time to Change and Other Poems. London : Fortune Press, 1952.

Sixty Poems. Bombay : The Strand Book Shop, 1953.

The Third. Bombay : The Strand Book Shop, 1958.

The Unfinished Man. Calcutta : Writers Workshop, 1960.

The Exact Name. Calcutta : Writers Workshop, 1965.

Hymns in Darkness. Delhi : Oxford University Press, 1976.

Latter-Day Psalms. Delhi : Oxford University Press, 1982.

Collected Poems 1952-1988. Delhi : Oxford University Press, 1989.

(ii) Non-Poetical Works

(a) *Plays*

Three Plays. Calcutta : Writers Workshop, 1969.

Song of Deprivation. *Enact*, July 1969.

Don't Call It Suicide : A Tragedy. Madras : Macmillan, 1994.

(b) *Essays*

"Ideas and Modern Poetry." *Indian Writers in Conference*. Bombay : The PEN All India Centre, 1964, pp. 48-54.

"T.S. Eliot : A Personal Review." *Quest*, 45 (March-April 1965), 17-22.

"Naipaul's India and Mine." *Imprint*, 1965. Also in Jussawalla, Adil. Ed. *New ,Writing in India*. Harmondsworth : Penguin, 1974, pp. 71-90.

"Shri Aurobindo on Poetry." *The Times of India* (Sunday), 23 July 1972, p. 9.

"Should Poetry Be Read to Audiences." *The Statesman* (Sunday Magazine), 27 August 1972, p. 2.

"Cross-Cultural Encounter in Literature." *The Indian Pen*, 43, 11-12 (November-December 1977), 4-8.

"What is Indian in Indo-English Poetry?" *Osmania Journal of English Studies*, 19 (1983), 49-58.

"The Heritage of India: A personal Statement." *Setu*, 1, 3 (1985), 71-73.

Selected Prose. Delhi : Oxford University Press, 1992.

"Poetry in the Time of Tempests." *The Times of India* (Sunday), 29 June 1997, II.

SECONDARY SOURCES

Belliappa, Meena. "Ezekiel's 'Poet, Lover, Birdwatcher' : An Explication." *The Miscellany*, 46, July-August (1971), 25-44.

Beston, John B. "An Interview with Nissim Ezekiel." *World Literature Written in English*, 16, 1 (April 1977), 87-94.

Bharucha, Nilufer E. "In Conversation with Nissim Ezekiel." In Bharucha, N.E. & Nabar, Vrinda, Eds. *Mapping Cultural Spaces*. New Delhi : Vision Books, 1998, pp. 11-40.

Birjepatil, J. "Interior Cadences : The Poetry of Nissim Ezekiel." *Literary Criterion*, 12, 2-3 (1976), 198-212.

Chari, A.J. "Poetics of the City." *Osmania Journal of English Studies*, 17 (1981), 105-21.

——. "Nissim Ezekiel," *Contemporary Literary Criticism*, 61 (1988), 90-113.

Coppola, Carlo. "Nissim Ezekiel's Most Recent Poems" in Parameswaran, Uma, Ed. *The Commonwealth in Canada*. Calcutta : Writers Workshop, 1984, pp. 158-73.

Das, B.K. *The Horizon of Nissim Ezekiel's Poetry*. New Delhi : B.R. Publishers, 1995, pp. 119.

De Souza, Eunice. "Notes" on Ezekiel's *The Unfinished Man*." Calcutta : Writers Workshop, 1969, pp. 16.

——. "A Poet's Journey." *The Times of India* (Sunday), 16 April 1989, II.

Dwivedi, A.N. "Modernity in Nissim Ezekiel's Poetry." *World Literature Today*, Summer 1992, 432-34.

Dwivedi, S.C. Ed. *Perspectives on Nissim Ezekiel.* Allahabad : Kitab Mahal, 1989, pp. 280.

Edington, Norman Ross. "Nissim Ezekiel's Vision of Life and Death." *Journal of South Asian Literature*, 22, 2 (1987), 139-45.

German, Michael, "Nissim Ezekiel : Pilgrimage and Myth" in Naik, M.K. *et al.* Eds. *Critical Essays on Indian Writing in English.* Madras : Macmillan, 1968, pp. 136-51.

Journal of Indian Writing in English (Nissim Ezekiel Number), 14, 2 (July 1986), 1-136.

Journal of South Asian Literature (Nissim Ezekiel Number), 11, 3-4 (Spring-Summer, 1976), 1-282.

Karnani, Chetan. *Nissim Ezekiel.* New Delhi : Arnold-Heinemann, 1974, p. 192.

Kher, Indra Nath. "That Message from Another Shore : The Aesthetic Vision of Nissim Ezekiel." *Mahfil* (now, *Journal of South Asian Literature*), 8, 4 (1972), 17-28.

——. "Beside the Final Void : Nissim Ezekiel's *Sixty Poems.*" *Toronto South Asian Review*, 4, 2 (Fall 1985), 74-88.

Khullar, Ajit. "Old Psalms for New Times." *Indian Literature*, 103 (September-October 1984), 219-27.

King, Bruce, "Ezekiel and His Influence." *Modern Indian Poetry in English.* Delhi : Oxford, 1987, pp. 91-109.

——. "Nissim Ezekiel : 1948-1965" and "Ezekiel : Later Poems." *Three Indian Poets.* New Delhi : Oxford, 1991, pp. 20-37 and pp. 38-59.

Kohli, Suresh. "Interview with Nissim Ezekiel." *Mahfil* (now *Journal of South Asian Literature*), 8, 4 (Winter 1972), 7-10.

Kurup, P.K.J. "Voyage : 'The Self' in the Poetry of Nissim Ezekiel." *Contemporary Indian Poetry in English.* New Delhi : Atlantic, 1991, pp. 10-106.

Lal, Emmanuel N. "Nissim Ezekiel." *The Poetry of Encounter*. New Delhi : Sterling, 1983, pp. 65-95.

Lal, Vinay. "A No Mean Poet of the Mean." *Indian Literature*, 34, 4 (July-August 1991), 158-67.

McCutchion, David. "Examen de Midi." *The Miscellany*, 29 (October 1968), 71-73.

Mishra, Sanjit. "The Humanistic Aspect of Nissim Ezekiel's Recent Poetry" in Pandey, Mithilesh K. Ed. *Contemporary Indian Literature in English : A Humanistic Perspective*. Ludhiana : Kalyani Publishers, 1999, pp. 1-7.

Mohanty, Niranjan. "The Self Within the Self." *Panjab University Research Bulletin (Arts)*, 23, 2 (October 1992), 107-24.

——. "Indianization of English : Poetry of Nissim Ezekiel" in Pathak, R.S. Ed. *Indianization of Indian English Literature*. New Delhi : Bahri, 1994, pp. 92-99.

Naik, M.K. "The Tale is in the Sting." *Dimensions of Indian English Literature*. New Delhi : Sterling, 1984, pp. 35-40.

Narayan, Shyamala A. "Nissim Ezekiel's *Latter-Day Psalms* : A Study." *Journal of Indian Writing in English*, 13, 1 (January 1985), 31-38.

Narula, S.C. "Negative Affirmation in Nissim Ezekiel's *Hymns* and *Psalms*." *Ariel*, 14, 4 (October 1983), 57-71.

Pandey, Surya Nath. "The Nature of Ezekiel's Patria." *Panjab University Research Bulletin (Arts)*, 22, 2 (October 1991), 83-88.

——. "An Approach to Nissim Ezekiel's Poetry." *Odyssey*, 1 (1996), 107-14.

——. "Post-Colonial Gestures in Nissim Ezekiel's Poetry." *Studies in Contemporary Poets*. New Delhi : Atlantic, 1998, pp. 84-90.

——. (Ed.) *Nissim Ezekiel : Dimensions of a Poetic Genius*. Delhi : Doaba House, 1999, pp. 232.

——. "Nissim Ezekiel's 'Background' Casually' : Travails of Cultural Marginality" : *Studies in Humanities and Social Sciences*, 6, 1 (Summer 1999), 111-18.

Parthasarathy, R. "Foregrounding as an Interpretative Device in Ezekiel's "Night of the Scorpion." *Literary Criterion*, 11, 3 (Winter 1974), 38-44.

Pathak, R.S. "Nissim Ezekiel : Quest for Linguistic Identity." *Quest for Identity in Indian English Writing*, Vol. II New Delhi : Bahri, 1992, pp. 32-56.

Raghunandan, Lakshmi, *Contemporary Indian Poetry in English.* New Delhi : Reliance Publishing House, 1990, pp. 295.

Rahman, Anisur. *Form and Value in the Poetry of Nissim Ezekiel.* New Delhi : Abhinav, 1981, pp. 92.

Raizada, Harish, *Nissim Ezekiel : Poet of Human Balance.* Ghaziabad : Vimal Prakashan, 1992, pp. 196.

Rao, K. Raghvendra. "The Alienation Games : The Poetry of Nissim Ezekiel," in Naik, M.K. Ed. *Perspectives on Indian Poetry in English.* New Delhi : Abhinav, 1984, pp. 98-108.

Rao, R. Raj. *Nissim Ezekiel : The Authorized Biography.* New Delhi : Viking Penguin, 2000.

Saha, Subhas Chandra. "Ezekiel's Enterprise." *The Miscellany*, 40 (July-August 1970), 9-23.

Sharma, T.R. Ed. *Essays on Nissim Ezekiel.* Meerut : Shalabh, 1994, pp. 267.

Singh, Frank Birbal. "Interview with Nissim Ezekiel." *The Illustrated Weekly of India* 1986. Also in *Journal of South Asian Literature*, 22, 2 (Summer-Fall 1986), 130-38).

Singh, Satyanarayan. "Ramanujan and Ezekiel." *Osmania Journal of English Studies*, 7, 1 (1969), 67-75.

——. "Journey into Self : Nissim Ezekiel's Recent Poetry." *Osmania Journal of English Studies*, 13, 1 (1977), 29-43.

Sreenivasan, S. & V. Rajakrishnan. "Interview with Nissim Ezekiel." *Journal of Literature and Aesthetics*, 4, 4 (October-December 1984), 26-39.

Taranath, Rajeev & Meena Belliappa. *The Poetry of Nissim Ezekiel.* Calcutta : Writers Workshop, 1966, p. 19.

Verghese, C. Paul. "The Poetry of Nissim Ezekiel." *Indian Literature*, 15, 1 (March 1972), 63-75.

Walsh, William. "Two Indian Poets." *Literary Criterion*, 11, 3 (Winter 1974), 1-16.

——. "Small Observations on a Large Subject" in Naik, M.K. Ed. *Aspects of Indian Writing in English*. Madras : Macmillan, 1979, pp. 101-19.

Wieland, James. "Making Light of the Process : Nissim Ezekiel's Poetic Fictions" in Prasad, H.M. Ed. *Indian Poetry in English*. Aurangabad : Parimal, 1983, pp. 99-112.